McKinsey Quarterly

On the cover: Strategy and leadership in turbulent times

Strategy/Organization

2010
Number 1

Special report

Energy, Resources, Materials

The water imperative

Other features

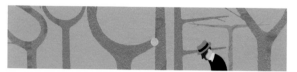

Departments

This Quarter

Rising to today's challenges

This issue of *McKinsey Quarterly* focuses on two of the most important challenges of the day for senior executives: decision making under uncertainty and the role of business in society. Many (though not all) denizens of the C-suite say that the financial crisis and the global recession it spawned have changed their assumptions about consumer behavior and competitive dynamics so much that a new managerial model is required. Our times, they argue, have generated a "new normal" that calls for a more agile approach to decision making—a theme that runs through the cover package of articles beginning on page 29.

The financial crisis has complicated the lives of senior executives in other ways too. The search for responsibility for the events that prompted the economic turmoil has led to the doors of the C-suite. It's no exaggeration to say that the reputations of many businesses and of the corporate world more broadly have taken a pounding. Regulators and consumers are raising fundamental questions about the role of business in society, and many companies seem to be searching for answers—and failing to find them. A recent McKinsey survey found that only 6 percent of C-level respondents said they thought senior executives were playing a leadership role in addressing social issues—the same share as in a 2007 survey.

Even before the crisis hit, executives at many forward-looking companies had begun to reflect on the role of their businesses in society, a movement sometimes referred to as corporate social responsibility, including the sustainability of business practices. These executives have done so not only in response to demands from stakeholders such as consumers and governments but also because they see business opportunities. Sustainability and business values are front and center in this issue's interviews with executives at Ford Motor Company, Unilever, Nestlé, and Rio Tinto and in its contributions from McKinsey consultants.

In the area of sustainability, a special report focuses on the increasingly serious challenge of water scarcity, a subject that only now is starting to receive the attention it deserves from governments and private enterprise. "The business opportunity in water conservation" looks at ways companies can not only cut costs by using water resources more efficiently but also create business opportunity from improving the water efficiency of other users. In these articles and interviews, we hope our readers will come away with a sense of how some of the world's biggest companies are thinking about—and acting on—what one might call the new normal of business in society.

Lenny Mendonca
Director, San Francisco

8

On Our Web Site

Now available on mckinseyquarterly.com

Interactives and videos

The future of capitalism: Building a sustainable energy future

In a collaboration between Duke University's Fuqua School of Business and McKinsey, a panel of experts and CEOs from leading energy companies debate the critical scientific, resource, and policy issues challenging energy sustainability today.

Enduring Ideas: The three horizons of growth

In this interactive presentation, Steve Coley, a director emeritus in McKinsey's Chicago office, describes the three horizons framework. Based on research into how companies sustain growth, this approach illustrates how to manage for current performance while maximizing future opportunities for growth.

Rebuilding the American dream: An interview with Pete Peterson

The quintessential business statesman reflects on a long career and the work needed to rebuild America's economic future.

Articles

Making the most of corporate social responsibility

For companies that see CSR as an opportunity to strengthen the business, the big challenge is execution. Smart partnering can provide a practical way forward.

Improving worker performance in the US government

Government leaders have the opportunity to improve the performance of their organizations. To do so they will need to harness the talents and motivation of their workforce.

Mastering sales force integration in a merger

Companies can seize the opportunity in mergers by involving employees and customers in the integration process, retaining critical staff, generating momentum by quickly winning key accounts, and serving the right customers in the right way.

Commercial real-estate lending: Finding economic profit in a difficult industry

While the industry ails, some commercial real-estate lenders thrive.

Conversation starter

The right way to invest in infrastructure

New thinking is needed to deliver the benefits of public-works spending and eliminate the waste.

Put our headlines on your page

Our widgets let you share the latest *Quarterly* headlines on your social network, blog, or personalized page. Show all headlines or just those for a single function. **mckinseyquarterly.com/widgets**

Surveys

Leadership through the crisis and after: McKinsey Global Survey results

Executives have markedly changed their leadership styles in the past year—but not their views on which ones will help companies most in the long term. Many of the most needed leadership styles, now and in the future, are those used more frequently by women than by men.

Tackling sociopolitical issues in hard times: McKinsey Global Survey results

The financial crisis has increased the public's expectations of business's role in society. Most companies have maintained or increased their efforts to address sociopolitical issues, and many have already derived better-than-expected benefits from doing so.

More from McKinsey

Join the conversation on What Matters

Join this discussion at:
whatmatters.mckinseydigital.com

McKinsey's *What Matters* convenes leading thinkers from around the world weighing in on topics from geopolitics to the credit crisis to health care that will shape our future. The newest topic looks at the dollar. It's been the world's reserve currency for the past century, but now it's showing signs of stress. Will it retain its status? And what happens if it doesn't?

Video and audio podcasts on iTunes

Download conversations with executives and authors in audio or video from iTunes.

mckinseyquarterly.com/itunes

Recent podcast:
Contemplating the future of capital markets

Join the *McKinsey Quarterly* community on Facebook

facebook.com/mckinseyquarterly

Follow us on Twitter

Receive notification of new articles by following **@McKQuarterly** on Twitter.

Letters to the Editor

Reader responses to articles in *McKinsey Quarterly*, 2009 Number 4

Think regionally, act locally:
Four steps to reaching the Asian consumer

The most successful global consumer enterprises are radically reshaping their organizations and business models to suit the region's rapidly evolving high-growth markets.

Where Asian consumers differ radically with their counterparts in other markets is in the area of sharing personal information: they are far more willing than those in other markets. This is opening tremendous possibilities for personalization, which is where marketers need to start focusing if they want to win in the long term. There needs to be a lot of attention paid to this area, considering the startling rate of proliferation of digital technologies such as mobile, where Asian markets are jump-starting and completely bypassing the learning-curve loop. The easy growth in Asia is hampering the development of personalized communications to some extent, but this will be a critical differentiator for successful companies in the long run.

Harpreet Singh Kaintel
Regional strategy director
ZenithOptimedia, Singapore

Increasing the energy efficiency of supply chains

The supply chains of many manufacturing sectors went global when oil was cheap; today, improving energy efficiency is a top concern for executives.

Traditionally, transport has been seen as a tactical and operational issue, and there are numerous examples of companies making changes of this nature that not only reduce the carbon footprint but also improve the bottom line—including the use of in-vehicle communications systems to avoid traffic congestion, driver education in ecodriving, and improved coordination and planning of shipments between facilities in order to boost the fill-rate of vehicles. A common denominator among these measures is that they all decrease the amount of CO_2 per ton-kilometer by decreasing overall fuel consumption.

At the same time, they have also made strategic changes to their supply chains that, in many cases, counteract the benefit of these measures. A typical strategic supply chain change involves reconfiguration in terms of number and location of production sites and warehouses. Decisions of this type determine the amount of ton-kilometers a supply chain generates. Over the past few decades, customers have been demanding shorter lead times, smaller order quantities, more frequent deliveries, and narrower delivery windows. Simultaneously, companies have sought to find economies of scale in their production, and, as a consequence, production plants and warehouses have become more dispersed. This development has led to an overall increase in the amount of ton-kilometers generated by companies' supply chains.

This illustrates why companies need to approach the issue of transport and the environment in a more holistic manner if they are to curb the problem of increasing CO_2 emissions. They must understand how to connect changes in ton-kilometers with changes in CO_2 emissions per ton-kilometer in order to shrink the carbon footprint of transport in their supply chains.

Christofer Kohn
Management consultant
UnitedLog, Stockholm, Sweden

Visit our Web site at mckinseyquarterly.com to read comments from our readers on these and other articles—or share your own.

A consumer paradigm for China

A more consumer-centric economy would allocate capital and resources more efficiently, generate more jobs, and spread the benefits of growth more equitably. It would also even grow more rapidly.

While I appreciate the economic analysis of China's need for domestic spending and consumption, absent from the analysis is whether China's current practices in manufacturing are sustainable in light of global warming, access to fossil fuels, and diminishing natural resources. Increasing consumption cannot be the sole solution to China's economic development. How does your analysis of economic growth and consumption take into account the impact of increased energy and water use on Chinese and global security?

Betsy Hands
State representative
Montana House of Representatives,
Missoula, MT USA

The article is enlightening and seems well researched. I, however, think it is written from a Western viewpoint that presupposes China should evolve in the image of Western economies. Societies that work well in the world are those that have evolved based on their culture and needs, not on copying economic and social practices from other nations. China's policy makers are best advised to determine the vision of society their people need, to learn from the rest of the world, and to fashion policies that will support that vision—to increase internal consumption in harmony with Chinese people's overall needs.

Joseph Ogbonna
Part owner
Ruuvand LTD, London, UK

China and the US: The potential of a clean-tech partnership

Only a collaboration between the world's two largest carbon emitters will create an environment where clean-energy technologies can thrive.

It is totally clear that the world's two largest polluters (one in aggregate and the other per capita) have to collaborate to make any progress in terms of emission reductions. However, the acknowledgement of emission reduction as a global problem is glaringly absent in this article. For example, it would be interesting to see how these two titans could learn from the real environmental leaders: Europe and Japan. As with US foreign policy, uni- or bilateralism will only cause more harm than benefit to the world.

Martin Lockstrom
Research associate
China Europe International Business School, Shanghai, China

I do agree that China and the US should build up a closer partnership on clean technologies and the low-carbon economy to confront common challenges, and take joint efforts to manage some key concerns like intellectual-property protection. However, I don't understand why in this article three clean technologies (electric vehicles, carbon capture and storage, and concentrated solar power) are chosen among many alternatives as must-have solutions. Frankly, I don't have much confidence in any of them and I can't help doubting that they conform with China's particular conditions.

Hazel Shao
Energy efficiency vice chairman
Independent Power Producers Forum,
Hong Kong

In Brief

Research and perspectives on management

Conversation Starter

Short essays by leading thinkers on management topics

Motivating people: Getting beyond money

Martin Dewhurst, Matthew Guthridge, and Elizabeth Mohr

Companies around the world are cutting back their financial-incentive programs, but few have used other ways of inspiring talent. We think they should. Numerous studies have concluded that for people with satisfactory salaries, some nonfinancial motivators are more effective than extra cash in building long-term employee engagement. Many financial rewards mainly generate short-term boosts of energy, which can have damaging unintended consequences.

Martin Dewhurst is a director in McKinsey's London office, where **Matthew Guthridge** is an associate principal and **Elizabeth Mohr** is a consultant.

A recent *McKinsey Quarterly* survey[1] underscores that the economic crisis provides a great opportunity for business leaders to reassess their incentives strategies. The respondents view three noncash motivators—praise from immediate managers, leadership attention (for example, one-on-one conversations), and a chance to lead projects or task forces—as no less or even more effective motivators than the three highest-rated financial incentives: cash bonuses, increased base pay, and stock or stock options (exhibit). The survey's top three nonfinancial motivators play critical roles in making employees feel that their companies value them, take their well-being seriously, and strive to create opportunities for career growth. These themes recur constantly in most studies on ways to motivate and engage employees.

There couldn't be a better time to reinforce more cost-effective approaches. Money's traditional role as the dominant motivator is under pressure from declining corporate revenues and increasing scrutiny by regulators and the general public. Our in-depth interviews with HR directors suggest that many companies have cut remuneration costs by 15 percent or more.

What's more, employee motivation is sagging throughout the world—morale has fallen at almost half of all companies, according to another McKinsey survey[2]—at a time when businesses need engaged leaders and other employees willing to go above and beyond expectations. Organizations face the challenge of retaining talented people. Strong talent management is also critical to recruit new ones who have been laid off from their employers or who feel disenchanted with them.

Even though overall reliance on financial incentives fell over the last 12 months, a number of companies curtailed their use of nonfinancial ones as well. Thirteen percent of survey respondents report that managers praise their subordinates less often, 20 percent that opportunities to lead projects or task forces are scarcer, and 26 percent that leadership attention to motivate talent is less forthcoming.

Why haven't many organizations made more use of cost-effective nonfinancial motivators at a time when cash is hard to find? One reason is probably because nonfinancial ways to motivate people require more time and commitment from senior managers. One HR director we interviewed spoke of their tendency to 'hide' in their offices—primarily reflecting uncertainty about the current situation and outlook. This lack of interaction between managers and their people creates a highly damaging void that undermines employee engagement.

However, some far-thinking companies are working hard to understand what motivates employees and to act on their findings. One global pharmaceutical company conducted

Exhibit: **It's not about the money**

Three nonfinancial incentives are even more effective motivators than the three highest-rated financial incentives.

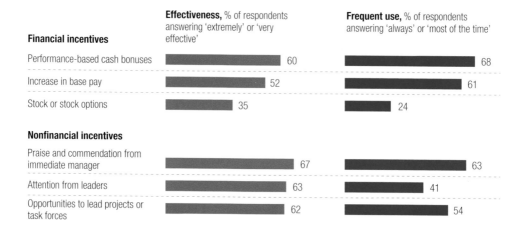

Financial incentives	Effectiveness, % of respondents answering 'extremely' or 'very effective'	Frequent use, % of respondents answering 'always' or 'most of the time'
Performance-based cash bonuses	60	68
Increase in base pay	52	61
Stock or stock options	35	24
Nonfinancial incentives		
Praise and commendation from immediate manager	67	63
Attention from leaders	63	41
Opportunities to lead projects or task forces	62	54

Source: June 2009 McKinsey global survey of 1,047 executives, managers, and employees from a range of sectors

Read what other people are saying at mckinseyquarterly.com, then join the conversation.

The big challenge for companies is to work equally as hard at understanding what satisfies employees as we do for customers. Businesses need to segment their workforces, identify which motivators really switch people on, and provide the right offer. This recession is truly going to be a moment of truth for leadership.

— Andrew Payne
Strategic relations development director,
Halcrow

While financial incentives will always be important, what troubles me is that companies are moving back so quickly to bonuses again. Did no learning take place from what happened on Wall Street?

— Neeru Biswas
Program director, The Asia Institute
SolBridge International School of Business

I can confirm that attention from top leaders works. I ran the suggestion scheme in a plant of the late Fokker Aircraft company. The best ideas that were worth implementing (about four to eight per year) were rewarded a net cash bonus of €6,000 to €10,000. But the picture in the company newsletter of the genius and the plant manager gathered round the idea at the shop floor, plus a break for coffee and cakes with closest colleagues, and above all the plant manager's genuine interest and appreciation was according to most of them the important part of their total reward.

— L. J. Lekkerkerk
Lecturer, *Radboud University Nijmegen*

a survey that showed that in some countries, employees emphasized the role of senior leadership; in others, social responsibility. The company is now increasing the weight of engagement metrics on its management scorecard so that they are seen as core performance objectives.

The top three nonfinancial motivators our survey respondents cited offer guidance on where management might focus. The HR directors we spoke with emphasized leadership attention as a way to signal the importance of retaining top talent. For example, a leading beverage company asked every executive committee member to meet with the critical people in their own product groups. 'One-on-one meetings between staff and leaders are hugely motivational,' explained an HR director from a mining and basic-materials company—'they make people feel valued during these difficult times.'

A chance to lead projects is a motivator that only half of the companies in our survey use frequently, although this is a particularly powerful way of developing their leadership capabilities. A company from

> Once again, top managers and executives say that nonfinancial incentives and rewards are the most effective motivating factors for their staff. Yet these same top people continue to award themselves huge salaries and unjustifiably large stock options and performance bonuses. Why do they think that nonfinancial rewards work for other people, but not for themselves? Perhaps, with appropriate acknowledgement of the Roman origins of the word 'salary,' we should take their views with a grain of salt!
>
> — Richard Rudman

> I would add that companies must communicate very clearly to employees. If the old programs were largely cash based, then a strong communication theme when restarting with a largely noncash recognition program would be the company's commitment to much more frequent, more timely, and more personal recognition for all employees (not just the elite, to whom bonus and stock programs are typically limited). This effort to make recognition more strategic and behavior based (on company values) as well as outcome based (achievement of strategic objectives) reinforces those behaviors you most want to see from all employees.
>
> — Derek Irvine
> Chief strategist, *Globoforce*

> Meaningful work, specific goals, celebrating success, and heartfelt and personal thank-yous work very effectively. The handwritten personal note is effective—even with younger generations who have never written or received a note—it's a total and very positive surprise.
>
> — Anne Murray-Randolph
> Assistant vice president for communications and special projects, *Yale University*

the beverages industry, for example, selected 30 high-potential managers to participate in a leadership program that created a series of projects designed and led by the participants.

With profitability returning to some geographies and sectors, we see signs that bonuses will be making a comeback: for instance, 28 percent of our survey respondents say that their companies plan to reintroduce financial incentives in the coming year. While such rewards have an important role to play, business leaders would do well to consider the lessons of the crisis.

A talent strategy that emphasizes the frequent use of the right nonfinancial motivators would benefit most companies in bleak times and fair. By acting now, they could exit the downturn stronger than they entered it.

[1] *McKinsey Quarterly* conducted the survey in June 2009 and received responses from 1,047 executives, managers, and employees around the world. More than a quarter of the respondents were corporate directors or CEOs or other C-level executives. The sample represents all regions and most sectors.

[2] "Economic Conditions Snapshot, June 2009: McKinsey Global Survey Results," mckinseyquarterly.com, June 2009.

The full version of this article is available on mckinseyquarterly.com.

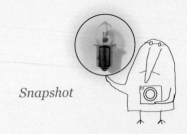

Snapshot

The new value at stake in regulation

Robin Nuttall and Sergio Sandoval

The expanding role of governments in the marketplace has become a hot topic in many executive suites around the world. But how much value is actually at stake from state intervention in the wake of the financial crisis of 2008? The answer, according to our analysis, is close to $800 billion a year of earnings before interest, taxes, depreciation, and amortization (EBITDA) worldwide—on top of around $2.8 trillion on the table before the crisis.

Regulation's impact varies by industry: half of the new value at stake is in banking and insurance, 15 percent in the automotive industry, and the remaining 35 percent scattered among other sectors. In banking and insurance, the crisis has added close to $400 billion to the industry EBITDA affected by government intervention and regulation, for a total of $970 billion (exhibit). This means that two thirds of the sector's profits are now at stake.

The huge regulatory impact of the crisis in just a few sectors doesn't mean that executives in other ones can relax. Telcos, transport and logistics companies, energy providers, retailers, pharma companies, and health care providers have long been subject to extensive government intervention. These industries continue to represent most of the regulatory value at stake around the world. Indeed, with a total of some $3.6 trillion a year on the table, an effective strategy for engaging government clearly has a place on the agendas of most CEOs.o

Robin Nuttall is a principal in McKinsey's London office, and **Sergio Sandoval** is a consultant in the Brussels office.

Exhibit: **Value at stake from regulation**

Government regulatory intervention since the economic crisis began has increased the value at stake across industries.

Estimated share of value at stake from government regulation, EBITDA[1]

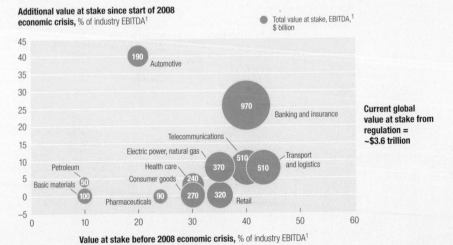

Additional value at stake since start of 2008 economic crisis, % of industry EBITDA[1]

Total value at stake, EBITDA,[1] $ billion

Current global value at stake from regulation = ~$3.6 trillion

Bubbles shown (y-axis value, total value at stake $ billion, label):
- Automotive: 190
- Banking and insurance: 970
- Telecommunications: 510
- Electric power, natural gas: 370
- Health care: 240
- Consumer goods: 270
- Transport and logistics: 510
- Retail: 320
- Petroleum: 90
- Basic materials: 50
- Pharmaceuticals: 100

Value at stake before 2008 economic crisis, % of industry EBITDA[1]

[1] Earnings before interest, taxes, depreciation, and amortization.

Source: Global Insight; interviews with experts; McKinsey analysis

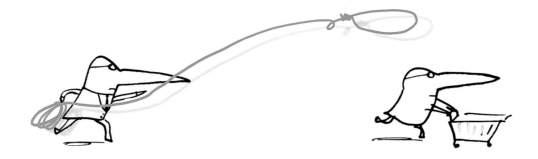

How the recession has changed US consumer behavior

Betsy Bohlen, Steve Carlotti, and Liz Mihas

While the downturn has certainly changed the economic landscape, it may also have fundamentally altered the behavior of numerous US consumers, who are now learning to live without expensive products. Many companies with strong premium brands are anticipating a rapid rebound in consumer behavior—a return to normality, as after previous recessions. They are likely to be disappointed.

New McKinsey research[1] found that, in any given category, an average of 18 percent of consumer-packaged-goods consumers bought lower-priced brands in the past two years. Of the consumers who switched to cheaper products, 46 percent said they performed better than expected, and the large majority of these consumers said the performance of such products was *much* better than expected. Consequently, 34 percent of the switchers said they no longer preferred higher-priced products, and an additional 41 percent said that while they preferred the premium brand, it 'was not worth the money.'

As a result, a growing number of consumers are now in play. The percentage up for grabs varies by category and depends on how many consumers switch from higher-priced brands, their experience with cheaper ones, and the way they revise their buying intentions. We found, for instance, that only 12 percent of beer buyers switched to cheaper brands. Of those, 31 percent said that their experience was more positive than they had expected, which means that only about 4 percent of customers are in play. Among buyers of cold and allergy medicines, however, we found that more than 20 percent tried a lower-priced option, and 48 percent of those consumers said the experience was better than expected. That means 10 percent of the people who buy cold and allergy medicines are now in play.

In industries where consumer shifts as small as 1 percent can severely dent the profitability of brands, these changes are significant enough to alter market dynamics and force brand leaders to respond. Earlier

Betsy Bohlen is a consultant in McKinsey's Chicago office, where **Steve Carlotti** is a director and **Liz Mihas** is a principal.

this year, P&G, for example, released Tide Basic, a cheaper version of its category-leading Tide laundry detergent, after Tide's sales began to decline as consumers switched to less expensive brands.

For companies attempting to address the change in consumer behavior, understanding the economic theory that explains why it is now shifting can help to inform decision making. Textbook theory posits that changes in the relationship between how much consumers are willing to pay, on the one hand, and their perception of the value they are receiving, on the other, underpins behavioral changes. As the exhibit shows, if consumers perceive enough value in a premium-brand product (Product A), they will favor it over the product of a more basic brand (Product B), despite the premium product's higher price. In a recession, though, consumers become less willing to pay more—the slope of the demand line flattens, and the preferences of some consumers begin to shift from Product A to Product B.

Normally, the premium-brand product would return to favor as the economy bounced back. But the central implication of our research is that even if the willingness of consumers to pay rebounds as the economy does, changes to their perceptions of the value of lower- and higher-priced products may fundamentally alter what they choose to buy. That's troubling for consumer-packaged-goods companies whose brands command premiums. If consumers see no legitimate reason to stick with such products, the premiums will slowly erode, and profit margins will shrink until category competition is determined mainly by price. A prime example is processed meats and sliced cheese, where the difficulty of demonstrating a product's superiority means that there's little scope for brands to differentiate by price. As a result, gross margins in these categories trail those of other branded foods.

Our experience in the consumer-packaged-goods sector suggests two priorities for companies addressing this fundamental shift in consumer behavior. The first is undertaking a situation assessment to understand a category's dynamics at a greater level of detail than can be achieved anecdotally or through survey research. Such an assessment involves analyzing purchasing behavior and motivations to determine how consumer requirements are changing and the effect of these changes on lower- and higher-priced products.

In our survey, for example, while most consumers said that the quality of the lower-priced brand was higher than expected, their precise reasons why varied. More than 33 percent of bottled-water users discovered that they no longer needed some of the benefits the higher-priced brand provided. Nearly 32 percent of facial-moisturizer consumers felt better about using the lower-priced brand than they had thought they would. What companies need is a fact-based understanding of the principles of typical consumer behavior to gauge how the willingness to pay for additional benefits has changed (illustrated in the exhibit by the slope of the line), the experience consumers have with products, and how perceptions of their value have changed.

The second step is developing action plans based on consumer dynamics and how well positioned products are for recovery. That means deciding where to position them in a way that will optimize the trade-off between prices and benefits, on the one hand, and margins and volumes, on the other. In the case of bottled water, the best response may be a lower-priced product that addresses the needs of consumers who no longer see the value in additional brand benefits. Yet decisions must also take into account the broader category strategy. We believe there's an opportunity to identify and increase participation in categories that have the potential to recover more rapidly and fully while minimizing exposure to those that have a lower chance of recovery or can recover only at the cost of brand or category economics. Looking at the exhibit, this means that brand portfolios should be aligned around categories with smaller changes in slope and where

---

Exhibit: **Changes in consumer behavior**
Consumers make trade-offs between perceived value and perceived price.

Before the downturn

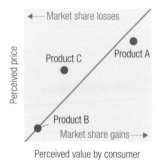

- Consumers are indifferent at any point on the diagonal 'demand line,' where perceived value and price are equal
- Product A is preferred because it is seen as a better value for the price
- Product C is at a disadvantage because its perceived value is too low given its perceived price

After the downturn

- - - Downturn effect

Change in willingness to pay

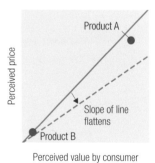

Change in perceptions

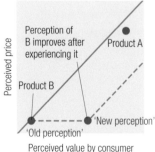

We welcome your com-
ments on these articles.
Please send them to
quarterly_comments@
mckinsey.com.

consumers have less positive experi-
ences with lower-priced products.

These steps are applicable beyond
consumer packaged goods. There's
evidence that the shift of consumers away from more expensive
products is a widespread trend.
In the consumer electronics industry,
for example, McKinsey research
found that 60 percent of consumers
were more interested in a core set
of product features at a reasonable
price than in the bells and whistles
of the latest and greatest technology
at a higher price.[2] Similarly, in the
building-products industry, there is
a trend away from premium-priced
design features and toward simpler,
more basic designs. Understanding this challenging shift in consumer
behavior is necessary for companies
to compete successfully. It represents an opportunity for those that
respond quickly and effectively
to differentiate themselves from
their peers. **o**

[1] The research, involving 2,672 US
consumers, was undertaken in August
2009.

[2] See Andre Dua, Lisa Hersch, and Manu
Sivanandam, "Consumer electronics gets
back to basics," mckinseyquarterly.com,
October 2009.

How innovators are changing IT offshoring

Michael Bloch, Dejan Boskovic, and Allen Weinberg

Michael Bloch is a director in McKinsey's Paris office, and **Dejan Boskovic** is a consultant in the New York office, where **Allen Weinberg** is a director.

In what has been a steady flow, global companies have moved portions of their IT operations—from software writing to the management of data centers—to a handful of large offshore players typically in India, the Philippines, and Eastern Europe. These are companies whose scale assured the lowest possible cost and best access to talent. But the model for how these services are delivered is shifting significantly. Some offshore leaders, as well as a phalanx of smaller, innovative players, are moving beyond low prices, guaranteeing service levels while raising the quality for even very complex tasks they perform. Global executives may want to rethink their current offshoring strategies so that they can benefit from a range of new opportunities.

Our 2008–09 survey of the global IT offshoring and outsourcing industry—covering 200 relationships among companies in Asia, Europe, and North America, including 65 of the Fortune 200 companies—shows that these rising suppliers have had a broad impact. In fact, they are changing the long-standing model for contracting offshore services, by focusing on the quality of services delivered rather than the usual benchmarks of costs per offshore hire. They are also developing the broader and deeper pools of talent that global clients increasingly demand and using progressive techniques to manage and retain this talent.

The most widely adopted model for delivering offshore services is called staff augmentation, but it is ceding ground to the more robust managed-services model. Under the traditional system, clients pay for each staff member a supplier adds to complete an IT contract—from the help desk operators who handle service problems to Java or mainframe software developers. Clients seek the lowest cost per head, which encourages stiff price competition among suppliers but gives the vendor limited incentive or accountability for the outcomes and quality, as no specific requirements or deliverables are defined in the contract.

Under the managed-services model, suppliers agree to deliver a specified capability or functionality with a desired level of service for a given price: for example, they contract to provide data center support for a year within certain volume and downtime parameters or to support production operations with clear, mutually agreed upon service levels. This model requires a higher level of trust, as clients cede more control to suppliers. Clients benefit by locking in the services they need without having to directly manage variable resource requirements at the offshore venue. Implementing these changes requires some additional work upfront by both suppliers and clients to redesign the roles and responsibilities of each throughout the product life cycle. It also means changing performance measures to fit the new responsibilities.

One pharma company moving to the new model invested considerable time upfront with its offshore supplier to document the underlying business processes and build internal capabilities (such as management tools, standardized work statements, and templates for service-level agreements) where it wanted a high level of support. Then the company created and managed a robust knowledge transfer process to ensure a successful and timely transition to the new delivery model. Although several months passed before the

benefits started to accrue, the quality of the supplier's work improved and the company shifted additional operations to it rapidly after the initial phase. Overall productivity rose.

Our survey shows that client organizations relying primarily on the managed-services rather than staff augmentation model reap great advantages: the best quality and most efficient delivery, the highest satisfaction levels, and the lowest attrition rates among their suppliers' employees (Exhibit 1).

While the economic slowdown has led to a degree of slackness in some of the normally tight markets for offshore labor, the suppliers in our survey report that they still face strong competition in hiring and retaining highly skilled talent. But the survey found that in some client–supplier relationships, attrition rates are low and satisfaction is high. In these relationships, talent is managed in a significantly different way.

The key to minimizing attrition is for clients to give suppliers wide-ranging authority to manage their teams locally in offshore locations. In part,

Exhibit 1: **The more satisfying model**

The managed-services model makes customers more satisfied.

Model used by IT services vendor	Overall customer satisfaction (on a scale of 1 to 5, where 1 = highly dissatisfied and 5 = highly satisfied)	Attrition, %	Vendor's ratio of IT head count offshored to those kept on-site
Staff augmentation is predominant model	3.2	15–30+	65 to 35 or worse
Evolving from staff augmentation to managed services	4.0	<20	70 to 30 or better
Managed services (time and material and fixed price) is predominant model	4.3	<10	80 to 20 or better

Source: 2008–09 McKinsey survey of the global IT offshoring and outsourcing industry

Exhibit 2: **Talent-management support**

Best practices can make employee attrition rates fall dramatically.

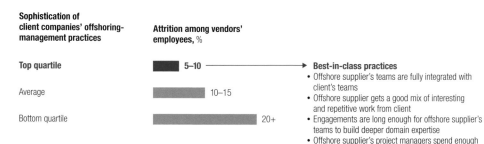

Sophistication of client companies' offshoring-management practices

Attrition among vendors' employees, %

Top quartile	5–10 →
Average	10–15
Bottom quartile	20+

Best-in-class practices
- Offshore supplier's teams are fully integrated with client's teams
- Offshore supplier gets a good mix of interesting and repetitive work from client
- Engagements are long enough for offshore supplier's teams to build deeper domain expertise
- Offshore supplier's project managers spend enough time at client's site in early phases of project
- Client brings onshore and offshore leaders together in same place to determine how to improve supplier's skills for complex business processes

Source: 2008–09 McKinsey survey of the global IT offshoring and outsourcing industry

We welcome your comments on these articles. Please send them to quarterly_comments@mckinsey.com.

that means working cooperatively with suppliers, developing their local team leaders, and letting them manage projects themselves. These best practices can make attrition rates fall dramatically (Exhibit 2). In one instance, a client closely integrated its domestic and offshore teams and sent its home-based employees to the offshore site, where they spent a substantial amount of time during the project's early phases. As part of the effort, the client brought onshore and offshore managers together to build the supplier's skills for a complex business process. Attrition rates dropped to 10 percent, from the 30 percent levels common in the offshoring industry. As one executive put it, 'Our philosophy shifted away from "supplier talent management and supplier attrition are supplier problems" to "proactively help them develop their talent and build a partnership."'

Clients can also help their suppliers to reduce attrition by mixing more challenging work (such as high-end development projects) with repetitive tasks (say, system maintenance, production support, or simple enhancements of previous work). A financial-services firm, for example, gave a supplier both the routine chore of maintaining and providing production support for finance P&L systems and the more demanding job of creating a next-generation derivatives platform. When more of this kind of challenging work comprises 30 to 40 percent of the workflow, our survey shows, attrition levels can fall to as little as half of those common in relationships where work is uniformly tedious. O

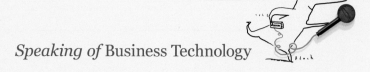

Speaking of Business Technology

An interview with MIT's Andrew McAfee

Roger P. Roberts

Web 2.0 technologies are changing the ways companies do business. In this excerpt from a video interview (available on mckinseyquarterly.com), Andrew McAfee—author of *Enterprise 2.0: New Collaborative Tools for your Organization's Toughest Challenges*—explains why he is optimistic about their potential to improve the way we work.

The *Quarterly*: *How do you get Enterprise 2.0 started in an organization?*

Andrew McAfee: One of my initial assumptions was after looking at the Web, where you can see the phenomenal growth of things like Facebook and Wikipedia and Flickr and YouTube and all that. I thought these technologies were essentially so cool that when you dropped them in an organization, people flocked to them. That was the assumption I carried around in my research. I very quickly had that overturned. This is not an overnight phenomenon at all. And while there are pockets of energy, getting mass adoption remains a pretty serious challenge for a lot of organizations.

I'm a fan of: deploy the tools, talk a little bit about what you want to have happen, and then find pockets of energy, highlight them, discuss them, show the good stuff that emerges. And also, signal from the top that this is what you want to have happen; when I see executives launch blogs, either internally or externally, I get pretty optimistic, because that's a very clear signal.

The *Quarterly*: *What is the CIO's role in encouraging Enterprise 2.0 and managing the risk?*

Andrew McAfee: A lot of them see their roles as essentially conservative. In other words, 'My job is to not increase the risk profile of this organization before everything else.' That's a legitimate concern, it's a legitimate job for the CIO, but all my experience so far tells me that Enterprise 2.0 *doesn't* increase the risk profile of an organization.

One really clever approach I heard was from Lockheed Martin, which is a large global aerospace and defense company. It has a lot of risk concerns, a lot of very legitimate security concerns. Their executives actually got pretty excited about Enterprise 2.0 and rolled out tools that very easily could be misused in this type of organization. When they rolled them out, though, they made sure that every kind of contribution could be flagged if it was inappropriate. That gave everyone a sense of calm that if something bad happens, all the eyeballs in this organization can help us find it. And they have a mechanism to flag it so that it comes to the attention of the compliance department.

Roger Roberts is a principal in McKinsey's Silicon Valley office.

'There's no technology—even these great new social technologies—that's a substitute for face time'

Andrew McAfee
Principal research scientist, Center for Digital Business at the MIT Sloan School of Management

I asked them how many posts or how many contributions had been flagged in the history of Enterprise 2.0. I believe the answer was zero.

The *Quarterly*: *What does this mean for middle managers?*

Andrew McAfee: If you're a middle manager who essentially views your job as one of gate keeping or refereeing information flows, you should be pretty frightened by these technologies, because they're going to greatly reduce your ability to do that. If you're someone who sees your job as managing people and fundamentally getting the human elements right that will lead your part of the organization to succeed, these technologies are not at all harmful to you. One of the things that we've learned is that there's no technology—even these great new social technologies—that's a substitute for face time. If you have another view of yourself, which is that you're someone who's responsible for output, these tools should be your best friend. Because all the evidence we have suggests that Enterprise 2.0 helps you turn out more and better products and actually is not a vehicle for time wasting or for chipping away at what you're supposed to be doing throughout the day.

The *Quarterly*: *How should companies measure the success of Enterprise 2.0?*

Andrew McAfee: I haven't come across people who have done our old-fashioned technology ROIs[1] and are happy with it. What I've seen instead is organizations that do a bit of thinking about: What challenge, what opportunity, are we trying to seize here? And then think about which exact technologies they can deploy to help them with that. So, for example, inside the US Intelligence Community, they had a really severe knowledge-sharing problem and a problem with locating expertise—throughout this huge, sprawling bureaucracy of 16 federal agencies—who knows a lot about the following topic. That was their huge challenge. The events of 9/11 made it very clear that that was a problem inside the intelligence community.

In their case, some of the most useful tools they've deployed have been simple tools like an intelligence community–wide Wiki and blogging environments where people can, the great phrase I've heard is, *narrate their work*. They can talk about what they know, what they're doing. If you add a bit of Google-flavored search on top of that, suddenly you have a very good way to find expertise, even in a very large, very decentralized organization. So that's the challenge they've faced.o

[1]Return on investments.

To watch a video of the full interview, visit mckinseyquarterly.com.

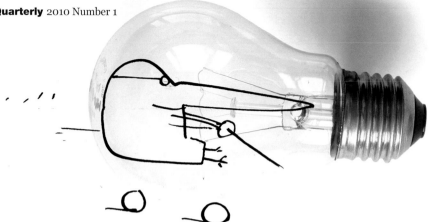

A new segmentation for electric vehicles

Nick Hodson and John Newman

Nick Hodson is a principal in McKinsey's San Francisco office, where **John Newman** is a consultant.

Global carmakers are trying to define a future market for electric vehicles. To reach beyond affluent, environmentally conscious, or technically enamored buyers, these companies will need to develop products that satisfy the consumers' main concern—good value for money. Given the current cost of energy storage, that is a considerable challenge.

A recent McKinsey study suggests that one way companies can achieve this goal would be to focus on tailoring battery-powered vehicles to the actual driving missions of specific consumers—that is, to the way they use their vehicles. Most existing gasoline-fueled cars, as well as many electric ones now on the drawing boards, are intended for multiple driving missions of differing lengths and speeds. By focusing on the specific driving missions of consumers, a company can match a vehicle's energy storage requirements to a consumer's particular needs and thus design more economic vehicles. It can also shape its brand and advertising messages and go-to-market strategies for such products more efficiently.

Our study, which focused on typical driving missions in the United States, examined the factors underlying the energy storage requirements, and thus the costs, of car batteries. We divided energy use into two major categories: the energy required, first, by the vehicles' physical characteristics (such as rolling resistance and mass) and, second, by the way the vehicles are used (such as driving distance, speed, and the frequency of stopping and starting). It is well understood that the addition of incremental energy storage increases an electric vehicle's cost substantially. (That isn't true for gas-fueled vehicles, since a larger gas tank is almost cost free.) But we found that the energy storage requirements of cars used for different missions could be vastly dissimilar, even if their size and total number of miles driven remained the same. Driving missions—much more than the size of vehicles—determine energy storage requirements.

Let's consider two common missions: driving around town and commuting. The latter's substantially higher energy storage requirements don't come mainly from the greater range required by a commuting car. Rather, the most significant factor is the higher average driving speed, and thus air resistance, encountered on freeways (Exhibit 1). The clear implication is that battery-powered vehicles suitable for the most energy-intensive driving missions, such as commuting, will overserve consumers who use their vehicles for shorter trips at lower speeds, such as running errands around town. Such vehicles won't deliver the right value at the right cost.

The reasons for focusing on the around-town market go well beyond shorter driving distances. Compared with vehicles powered by internal-combustion engines, battery-operated ones get better energy mileage (miles per kilowatt hour and thus per unit of energy storage) when driven at relatively low speeds on local streets, with a lot of stopping and starting (Exhibit 2). Representative driving missions include cars used in cities and in short-range suburban driving, as well as delivery vans and, perhaps, taxis. By our estimate, up to 38 million US households could purchase such a vehicle. The evidence is that they own at least two cars (so one can be used for more demanding activities), at least one has low annual mile-

age, and the households' annual incomes suffice for electric vehicles.

Battery electric vehicles aren't appropriate for all consumers or households, of course. Some require the extra range of plug-in hybrid-electric vehicles (PHEVs; cars and trucks that can run on electric power but also have small internal-combustion engines as backup). Here too a segmentation by driving mission is critical to make the economics of vehicles attractive. Exhibit 3 illustrates the operating cost of plug-in hybrids with distinct battery sizes suited to four representative driving missions, each of which involves different ranges of total annual miles and different distributions in trip lengths between each chance to charge the battery.

A segmentation by mission frees consumers from the need to pay for bigger cars and batteries than they actually need. Depending on how consumers use their vehicles, the battery size requirements (and thus upfront capital costs) and operating economics can vary quite substantially. The optimal battery size required for a plug-in hybrid driven around town is one-quarter that required by a sales

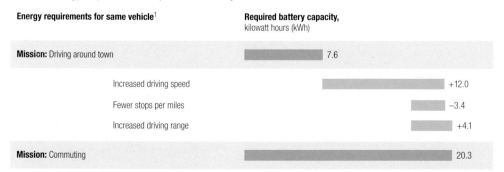

Exhibit 1: **The driving mission**
A car's energy requirements depend on the way it is used.

Energy requirements for same vehicle[1]	Required battery capacity, kilowatt hours (kWh)
Mission: Driving around town	7.6
Increased driving speed	+12.0
Fewer stops per miles	−3.4
Increased driving range	+4.1
Mission: Commuting	20.3

[1]Average figures; assumes level ground and standard driving conditions; does not include incremental storage for nonmotion activities (eg, heating, cooling, lights).

Exhibit 2: **Energy use differs**

Different driving missions require different amounts of energy.

Energy mileage for same vehicle, miles per kilowatt hour (kWh)

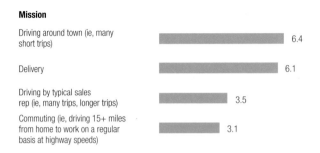

Mission	
Driving around town (ie, many short trips)	6.4
Delivery	6.1
Driving by typical sales rep (ie, many trips, longer trips)	3.5
Commuting (ie, driving 15+ miles from home to work on a regular basis at highway speeds)	3.1

Exhibit 3: **Segmenting by mission**

Plug-in hybrids can also benefit from segmentation based on the driver's mission.

Illustration of optimum battery sizes for plug-in hybrid-electric vehicle (PHEV), based on range in miles (all-electric driving)

Mission

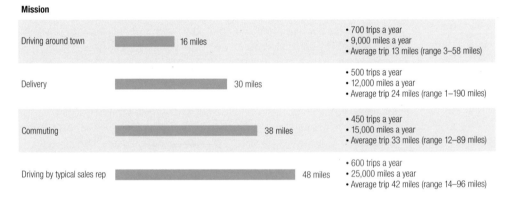

Mission		
Driving around town	16 miles	• 700 trips a year • 9,000 miles a year • Average trip 13 miles (range 3–58 miles)
Delivery	30 miles	• 500 trips a year • 12,000 miles a year • Average trip 24 miles (range 1–190 miles)
Commuting	38 miles	• 450 trips a year • 15,000 miles a year • Average trip 33 miles (range 12–89 miles)
Driving by typical sales rep	48 miles	• 600 trips a year • 25,000 miles a year • Average trip 42 miles (range 14–96 miles)

rep.[1] More important, the cost of the batteries is in proportion to their size—and at today's current battery cost of $750 or so per kilowatt hour, size can translate into significant savings, sometimes many thousands of dollars. One implication is that companies offering only a plug-in hybrid with, for example, 40 miles of all-electric range may be undercut by manufacturers of much less expensive vehicles with just 10 or 20 miles of electric range and only marginally higher operating costs. This is because it is much less expensive to use gasoline to cover infrequent trips that exceed a PHEV's all-electric range than to carry 'spare' battery capacity.

Focusing on designing and selling battery-powered vehicles to segments with specific driving missions also allows carmakers to articulate the values clearly to target buyers and to focus distribution strategies. While some automakers are taking this approach, many others are attempting to design vehicles that satisfy the needs of 95 percent of all customers. Our research suggests that these carmakers should be thinking in radically new ways about market segmentation. o

[1] Of course, vehicles must meet other on-board energy requirements (such as heating and cooling), which could raise the cost of the battery. The analyses here do not consider this issue explicitly.

Artwork by Serge Bloch/ Marlena Agency.

We welcome your comments on these articles. Please send them to quarterly_comments@ mckinsey.com.

On the cover:

Strategy and leadership in turbulent times

Artwork by Bill Butcher

Adapting to new realities

All things considered, Bill Ford has had a pretty good crisis. As US auto sales plunged from roughly 16 million vehicles in 2007 to 10 million in 2009, and Chrysler and GM landed in the arms of the government, Ford Motor Company stayed independent, even scratching out a billion-dollar operating profit during the third quarter of 2009. Ford doesn't know what comes next—'I think it would be the height of arrogance for me to try to anticipate any seismic changes,' he says—but neither is he betting on a return to normal. 'One of the lessons we've learned,' says Ford, 'is that we have to get our breakeven point down so that no matter what happens to the industry worldwide, we can be successful.'

That determination to control one's destiny, even in the face of profound uncertainty and massive shifts away from pre-crisis norms, runs through a series of recent McKinsey interviews with CEOs and other top executives. Blackstone Group cofounder Pete Peterson speaks of 'significantly less leverage, a tough market to raise substantial funds,' and a shift in 'the center of gravity of the private-equity business from financial engineering to operational improvements.' Surveying the consumer landscape, Unilever CEO Paul Polman says he 'clearly sees different consumer behaviors coming out of this recession'— among them, delays in big-ticket purchases and more frugal lifestyles, with less spending on 'discretionary items.' And Estée Lauder chief strategy officer Peter Jueptner concedes that his organization has 'stopped predicting growth rates,' opting instead for targets linked to unknowable macroeconomic realities: 'What you can do is say you're going to grow by, say, 1 percent ahead of whatever the market growth will be.'

Against this backdrop of change and uncertainty, one thing is crystal clear for executives: the post-crisis era—or the new normal, as many call it—requires an approach with far greater flexibility and a different way of working among members of the top team. McKinsey's Lowell Bryan calls it dynamic management. London Business School professor Don Sull emphasizes the importance of organizational agility. Estée Lauder's Jueptner stresses adaptability. The labels are less important than the message: embrace the ambiguity of the new environment; continually revisit plans and rethink assumptions, whether they are long held or only months old; and build an organization that can capitalize on the unexpected.

In the following package, we lay out several ideas for beginning that process. Bryan's 'Dynamic management: Better decisions in uncertain times' suggests new ways for senior executives to surface issues, make decisions, and escape traditional budgeting cycles. In 'Navigating the new normal,' four chief strategy officers describe the breakneck pace of planning these days and the 'indisputables' (to borrow a term from Visa CSO Niki Manby) that have come under attack. Next, Don Sull reminds us that market turbulence was on the rise well before the financial crisis and suggests how some companies have already built—and how others can foster—the agility needed to respond through well-thought-out ways of spotting and probing for opportunities, reallocating resources, and mitigating risk. Finally, Derek Dean describes the emotions unleashed as deeply ingrained assumptions are upended and suggests ways for CEOs to help their senior teams overcome the fear, denial, and mental blocks that can impede action.

Of course, cultivating the new management mind-set that all this implies is far from the only thing on the agenda of top management today. But at a moment when the pressure on executives in the C-suite is as great as it's been in a very long while, taking the time to rethink how they collaborate, establish priorities, and make their organizations more nimble just might be the most important thing of all. o

Dynamic management:
Better decisions in uncertain times

Companies can't predict the future, but they can build organizations that will survive and flourish under just about any possible future.

Lowell Bryan

The economic shock of 2008, and the Great Recession that followed, didn't just create profound uncertainty over the direction of the global economy. They also shook the confidence of many business leaders in their ability to see the future well enough to take bold action.

It's not as if we don't know how to make good decisions under uncertainty. The US Army developed scenario planning and war gaming in the 1950s. And advanced quantitative techniques, complete with decision trees and probability-based net-present-value (NPV) calculations, have been taught to MBA students since the 1960s. These approaches are extraordinarily valuable amid today's volatility, and many well-run companies have adopted them, over the years, for activities such as capital budgeting.

Here's the challenge: coping with uncertainty demands more than just the thoughtful analysis generated by these approaches (which, in any event, are rarely employed for all the business decisions where they would be useful). Profound uncertainty also amplifies the importance of making decisions when the time is right—that is to say, at the moment when the fog has lifted enough to make the choice more than a crap shoot, but before things are clear to everyone, including competitors.

Lowell Bryan is a director in McKinsey's New York office.

Over the past year or so, progressive strategists have been undertaking noble experiments (such as shorter financial-planning cycles) while dropping the pretense that they can make reasonable assumptions about the future (for some examples, see "Navigating the new normal: A conversation with four chief strategy officers," also in this package). My sense, though, is that achieving truly dynamic management will prove elusive for most organizations until they can figure out how to get their senior leadership (say, the top 150 managers) working together in a fundamentally different way. The knowledge, skill, and experience of these leaders make them better suited than anyone else to act decisively when the time is right. Such executives are also well placed to build the organizational capabilities needed to surface critical issues early and then use the extra lead time to gather intelligence, to conduct the needed analyses, and to debate their implications.

The specifics of how companies should build these muscles will of course vary. Well-run organizations—particularly those accustomed to using stage-gate-investment approaches for activities such as oil exploration, venture capital investment, and new-product development—may find that moving toward a more dynamic management style requires a few relatively small, though collectively significant, shifts in their operating practices. Others may find the necessary changes, which include migrating away from rigid, calendar-based approaches to budgeting and planning, more wrenching. What I hope to do in this article is to lay out some core principles that will help either kind of company make the passage of time an ally rather than a challenge.

Focusing on pivotal roles
A ship has a captain with a single mind. The "captain" of a large, complex modern corporation, however, is likely to be dozens, if not hundreds, of people. Aligning those pivotal leaders so that they can steer the company in response to changing conditions is a major challenge for most organizations.

An essential first step is simply to define who occupies the pivotal roles. Some companies may have just a few; others 20, 150, or even more. On the one hand, the smaller the number, the easier it is to have the intensity of interaction needed to make critical decisions effectively and collaboratively. On the other hand, the number must be large enough so that the people involved in decision making can collectively gain access to the full spectrum of knowledge embedded in a company's people and its relationships with other organizations. You'll never get perfect coverage, but if you wind up saying with any frequency, "We're flying blind on this topic without perspective from X," it's a good bet that you've kept the group too small.

Since determining what to do under uncertainty usually requires careful debate among many people across the entire company, you need processes and protocols to determine how issues are raised, how deliberation is conducted, and how decisions are made. You also need to clearly lay out the obligations of managers, once the debate and decision making is over, to put their full weight behind making the resulting actions successful.

I wish there were one-size-fits-all protocols for getting the smart, talented people who occupy pivotal roles (and who are accustomed to making decisions through a hierarchy) to work effectively with colleagues in collectively steering the ship. But the hard truth is that what works in one organization and among one set of individuals may not work in others. Since the move toward more dynamic management changes power relationships and the prerogatives of senior executives, a company's organizational, cultural, and political norms have a major influence on the ease of transition. (The more hierarchical and less collaborative the organization, for example, the bigger the challenge.) The best I can do is to suggest a few general approaches—whose implementation often looks quite different in different types of organizations—for helping the individuals occupying pivotal roles to work together in new ways.

> Many managers are reluctant to surface emerging issues early, because they fear being perceived as someone who is weak, or who cries wolf

Learning by doing

If you require managers to use decision-making-under-uncertainty techniques (such as scenario planning, decision trees, and stage gating) to make actual decisions, they will quickly learn how to think differently about the future. And if you have them apply these tools in teams involving executives from diverse corners of the organization, they will gain a greater appreciation for the power of collective insight in volatile times, when information, almost by definition, is fragmentary and fast moving.

Workshop-based adult-learning techniques

Executives can develop new mind-sets and skills, particularly to improve their ability to manage through the ambiguity and complexity inherent in today's environment. Some companies have made progress by developing case studies based upon potential decisions they will shortly be facing and then using facilitators and friendly colleagues to get leaders used to surfacing and debating alternative courses of action. Others have found war gaming useful for illustrating the cost of basing decisions on seemingly reasonable assumptions when events are moving quickly.

Performance measurement

Companies need to hold their managers not just individually but also mutually accountable for their actions. This means evaluating how effectively executives contribute to the success of others. For example, how effective are executives at identifying the company's critical issues, even when such issues fall outside their areas of responsibility? And how proactively do executives provide their colleagues with intelligence, knowledge, and advice? Peer-assessment techniques often are invaluable in measuring collaborative behavior.

Just-in-time decision making

Much of the art of decision making under uncertainty is getting the timing right. If you delay too much, opportunity costs may rise, investment costs may escalate, and losses can accumulate. However, making critical decisions too early can lead to bad choices or excessive risks. And making hasty decisions under time pressure or economic duress allows little room to undertake detailed staff work or to engage in careful debate. Here are a few suggestions for companies trying to create competitive advantage from their ability to manage the passage of time decisively.

Surfacing critical issues

Most companies are accustomed to identifying major internal issues, such as whether to build a business, divest an asset, or lay off people. What's harder—and has become increasingly important over the past year or so—is the early surfacing of opportunities and threats arising out of external events such as dramatic shifts in demand, competitive behavior, industry structure, regulation, or the macroeconomic environment.

A commonsense approach to identifying such issues early is to poll, regularly, all of the company's top managers to get them to identify critical issues they see emerging. Each manager should provide a rationale for why any issues raised are critical. A small team of senior executives should review all such issues, designating some as critical and highlighting others for continued tracking. As time passes, some of these other issues may become critical; others may become less relevant and disappear from the list.

One challenge: many managers are reluctant to surface emerging issues early, because they fear being perceived as someone who is weak, or who cries wolf. A well-designed performance-management system, though, can ensure that the personal risk of surfacing critical issues late is much greater than the risk of raising them too early.

Performing the necessary staff work

If a critical issue is surfaced early, there is usually time enough to use proven problem-solving approaches to making decisions under uncertainty. Decision trees, for example, help managers think about the structuring and sequencing of their decisions. Probabilistic modeling is useful for understanding the economic consequences of potential outcomes. Breaking big decisions into smaller, well-sequenced ones (the goal of stage-gate investing) helps organizations move forward without taking excessive risks. And building scenarios helps you gain perspective on your critical issues. If a particular decision produces favorable outcomes under all scenarios, it becomes a "no regrets" move justifying bold action. On the other hand, if a particular scenario is improbable, but the negative consequence (if

Five scenario traps to avoid

Charles Roxburgh

Scenarios enable the strategist to steer a course between the false certainty of a single forecast and the confused paralysis that often strikes in troubled times. But they can also set traps for the unwary.

1. Don't let scenarios muddy your communications

The former CEO of a global industrial company once suggested that scenarios are an abdication of leadership. His point was that a leader has to set a vision for the future and persuade people to follow it. Great leaders do not paint four alternative views of the future and then say, 'Follow me, although I admit I'm not sure where we are going.'

You can use scenarios without abdicating your leadership responsibilities, but you should not communicate with the organization via scenarios. You cannot stand up in front of it and say, 'Things will be good, bad, or terrible, but I am not sure which.' Winston Churchill's remarks about British aims in World War II— 'Victory at all costs, victory in spite of all terror, victory however long and hard the road may be'—are instructive. By insisting only on the final outcome, Churchill was not refusing to acknowledge that a wide range of conditions might exist. He was setting forth a goal that he regarded as what we would call 'robust under different scenarios.' He was acknowledging the range of uncertainties ('however long and hard the road may be'), and he resisted overoptimism.

2. Don't use too narrow a set of outcomes

One of the more dangerous traps of using scenarios is that they can induce a sense of complacency, of having all your bets covered. In this regard, at least, they are not so different from the value-at-risk models that left bankers feeling that all was well with their businesses— and for the same reason. Those models induced a false sense of security with regard to the potentially catastrophic effects of an event with a 1 percent probability. Creating scenarios that do not cover the full range of possibilities can leave you similarly exposed.

You can test the breadth of your scenario set by identifying extreme events—low-probability, high-impact outcomes—from the past 30 or 40 years and seeing whether your set contains a comparable scenario. Don't be trapped by the recent past. We are typically too optimistic going into a downturn and too pessimistic on the way out. No one is immune to this trap, including professional builders of scenarios. When heading into a downturn, always push your pessimistic scenario beyond what feels comfortable. When in the downturn, create a scenario more optimistic than any you feel you can reasonably expect.

Charles Roxburgh is a director in McKinsey's London office.

it happens) is large, you need to build contingency plans (see sidebar, "Five scenario traps to avoid").

If companies tried to make all or even most of their important decisions in this way, the costs could be prohibitive, and there wouldn't be enough management bandwidth available to do anything but debate issues. Employing a materiality test, such as whether 1 or 2 percent of a company's future earnings are at stake, is therefore vital. In a typical large company, this may mean no more than two or three dozen such issues in any given year.

3. Don't chop the tails off the distribution

In our experience, when people running businesses are presented with a range of scenarios, they tend to choose one or two immediately to the right and left of reality as they experience it at the time. Executives regard extreme scenarios as a waste of time because 'they won't happen' or, if they do, 'all bets are off.' When leaders ignore the outer scenarios and spend their energy on moderate improvements or deteriorations from the present, they leave themselves exposed to dramatic changes—particularly on the downside.

4. Don't discard scenarios too quickly

Sometimes the most interesting and insightful scenarios are the ones that initially seem the most unlikely. This raises the question of how long you should hold on to a scenario. Scenarios should be treated dynamically. Depending on the level of detail they aspire to, some might have a shelf life numbered only in months. Some you may keep and reuse over a period of years. Others you will look at, only to find they have become irrelevant. To retain some relevance, a scenario must be a living thing. You don't get a scenario right—you keep it useful. Scenarios get better if you revise them over time. When dropping scenarios, it is useful to add one for each that you discard. You want to maintain a suite of roughly the same

number at any given time. A scenario set should always contain at least four alternatives: show people three and they always pick the middle one. Four forces them to discover which way they lean.

5. Remember when to avoid scenarios altogether

Finally, bear in mind the sole instance in which you will not want to use scenarios: a situation in which uncertainty is so great that you cannot reliably build one at any level of detail. Just as scenarios help avoid groupthink, they can also generate a groupthink of their own. If everyone thinks the world can be categorized into four boxes on a quadrant, you might find that an organization has convinced itself that only four outcomes or kinds of outcomes can happen. That's very dangerous. You don't want to persuade yourself that you have identified all the reasonable scenarios when quite different possibilities are out there.

The full version of this article is available on mckinseyquarterly.com.

Changing how decisions are made

Few companies are organized to get just-in-time managerial alignment for even a few issues a year, let alone two or three dozen. Gaining alignment among pivotal decision makers requires them to spend time together (in person, by phone, or in videoconferences) to surface emerging issues, share information, debate issues, and make timely decisions. How much time is needed for such meetings will, of course, vary with the company and its circumstances but is likely to be in the range of two to three days a month.

The only way to make this happen is to redesign the corporate calendar, along with corporate processes and protocols for how the meetings are conducted (including their length, decision-making roles, and required attendees). The redesign should encompass the creation of processes that enable the rapid surfacing and formal designation of issues considered critical. In addition, some companies have found it helpful to create a situation room—a physical place manned by support staff and connected electronically to people who can't be physically present—to serve as a hub to mobilize the information needed to enable debate to take place in real time among the appropriate decision makers.

Rethinking corporate budgeting processes

Everything I've been describing flies in the face of management practices that have proven invaluable at many companies for nearly a century. Fixed annual planning and budget processes are antithetical to timely strategy setting and decision making.

Yet it's important to recall why we have them: they enable the efficient delegation of authority between managers and subordinates. In return for the freedom to make decisions and allocate resources, the subordinate contracts through the budget to deliver expected results. The managers of a large company make tens of thousands of operating decisions every day, and if all of them required constant deliberations up and down the chain of command and across the organization, it would grind to a halt.

Jettisoning budgeting, therefore, is hardly an option—though it may have seemed reasonable at points over the past year, since most of the budgets produced in late 2008 for 2009 proved worthless (as did most companies' earnings guidance to stock analysts). What this underscores is a basic problem with budgets: if developments in the marketplace are sufficiently different from the assumptions used in budgeting, managers can't make their numbers no matter what they do. At best, by the time these developments have surfaced, most of the lead time needed to address the emerging issues has been exhausted. At worst, the company faces a crisis after being weakened by the hidden costs of all of the short-term actions (such as maintenance cutbacks for manufacturers or excessive risk taking for financial institutions) undertaken by managers endeavoring to make their numbers.

So what's the answer? Many better-run companies have already adapted the budgeting process to make it more flexible. A large number use a base case, an optimistic case, and a pessimistic case to allow for a range of outcomes. More important, a significant percentage of companies now use rolling budgets to keep their plans current. These approaches aren't foolproof—many companies fall into the trap of using too narrow a range (such as plus or minus 5 percent), and even companies that use rolling budgets usually do so only by making small incremental adjustments, quarter to quarter, to the base case. Nonetheless, in a relatively stable environment, these approaches are a significant step forward.

But even rolling budgeting may not be enough to prepare you for a macroenvironment where you are unsure whether you will be seeing, over the next couple of years, a rapid return to global growth, an extended period of anemic growth, or a double-dip recession.

One alternative: move to a semiannual budgeting and financial-planning cycle where you make budget "contracts" for a 6-month, rather than annual, time period and undertake robust, scenario-based financial-contingency planning for the period from 6 to 24 months in the future. That approach allows companies both to continue using budgets that hold people accountable for the immediate future and to shift toward contingency budgets at the end of 6 months should the circumstances warrant a change of direction. I believe many companies will find that a semiannual budgeting process works better than either an annual approach, which is based upon an unrealistic year-long budget-contracting horizon, or a quarterly update, which requires almost continuous rebudgeting.

Related articles on mckinseyquarterly.com

Leading through uncertainty

How managers should approach a fragile economy

Setting strategy in the new era: A conversation with Lowell Bryan and Richard Rumelt

Another valuable and potentially complementary approach is to have even 6-month budgets and the results reported against them automatically adjusted for "uncontrollables." That is, to improve

accountability you can restate both budgets and results after the fact to remove, automatically, variances caused by macroeconomic uncontrollables such as interest rates, commodity prices, and currency movements. This approach can help senior leaders eliminate uncontrollable losses and windfall gains, thereby holding managers accountable for their performance in the marketplace rather than for whether the macroeconomy makes them lucky or unlucky.

Finally, many if not most companies will also find that they need to carve out discretionary budgets and staff to support just-in-time decision making. These budgets should be sufficient not just to support the needed staff work but also to provide the resources needed to begin implementing the decisions until they (and their financial implications) can be formally built into budgets.

• • •

We welcome your comments on this article. Please send them to quarterly_comments@mckinsey.com.

Companies can't control the weather, but they can design and build a ship, and equip it with a leadership team, that can navigate the ocean under all weather conditions. Organizations that become more flexible and skillful at making critical decisions when the timing is right have enormous opportunities to capture markets and profits from companies that persist in managing as if the future business environment is reasonably predictable.o

Navigating the new normal:

A conversation with four chief strategy officers

Allen P. Webb

Executives of Boeing, Estée Lauder, Smith International, and Visa describe an environment in which setting strategy has·become more complex and business assumptions that once seemed indisputable are coming into question.

| **Discussion participants:** | **Peter Jueptner,** Senior vice president, strategy and new business development, Estée Lauder | **Niki Manby,** Head of global corporate strategy, Visa | **Rik Geiersbach,** Vice president, corporate strategy, Boeing | **Peter Pintar,** Vice president, corporate strategy and development, Smith International |

Allen Webb is a member of *McKinsey Quarterly's* board of editors.

Are we experiencing a conventional economic cycle? Or did the financial crisis of 2008 and subsequent global economic downturn mark the beginning of a "new normal" characterized by fundamental changes in the use of leverage, trajectory of globalization, nature of consumption patterns, and appetite for risk-taking? Few, if any, members of the C-suite are better positioned to answer these questions than chief strategy officers, who typically find themselves on the hook for identifying tectonic shifts in the competitive landscape, and for predicting the future.

In early October, 2009, the CSOs of Boeing, Estée Lauder, Smith International, and Visa gathered to discuss what has and hasn't changed over the past year. While they didn't agree on everything, the four executives painted a collective picture of an environment in which setting strategy has become more complex: planning cycles are shrinking, future growth trajectories are harder to predict, and business assumptions that once seemed indisputable are now coming into question. What's more, the rapid pace of economic events is challenging CSOs in their efforts to focus on the long term, and to keep the organization and its processes well-aligned with shifting strategic priorities. What follows is an abridged summary of their discussion, which was moderated by McKinsey's Allen Webb.

The *Quarterly*: *Let's start by going around the table and asking whether we are indeed in a "new normal," and, if so, what it looks like.*

Peter Pintar: I don't think we are. I think we're coming off of something that was abnormal. It was really a speculative boom in the 2000s. Whatever normal is coming afterwards isn't going to look at all like the normal we've experienced in the last decade. The discussion around a new normal is ultimately a discussion around the shape and the timing of economic recovery.

We're in the middle of a downcycle. How rapidly we come out of that is really what this debate is about, as opposed to whether we're going to be entering a new and different restructured global economy. For those reasons, my sense is the phrase "new normal" isn't appropriate.

Niki Manby: It is a bit of a trick question, because as a strategist, conceding that there's something you weren't prepared for is not something you want to do!

That said, I do recognize a shift in much our strategy work. We generally looked to what I would call the "indisputables" that will carry us forward. When I think of "new normal," a constant that I see across industries is that it's difficult to find those indisputables. That does in fact feel very new.

The *Quarterly*: *What were some of the indisputables that you used to feel like you could count on that you can't now?*

Niki Manby: One of the indisputables that I believe is being tested is how consumers spend. We see a huge shift to debit as opposed to credit products. And there's one causal factor, which is, of course, our recent credit crunch.

Peter Jueptner: I think a lot of the consumer discussion we have is around North America. You could argue that from a global perspective, the new normal in North America is actually normal for a lot of other geographies. I think it's more of a normalization of the American consumer to what we've previously seen in other, more mature markets.

And then of course you have the emerging markets—markets, not just in Asia—where in our business at least, throughout the recession, we had double-digit growth—but also Latin America. I was just in Brazil. It's amazing. People are very, very optimistic there. We've shifted some of our resources into the more rapidly growing markets while we're adapting to the new environment in North America. We've also, by the way, stopped predicting growth rates. It's very hard to predict in these times how much the market will grow. What you *can* do is say you're going to grow by, say, 1 percent ahead of whatever the market growth will be.

Peter Pintar: Is that approach a function of this dysfunction that we've come through, or did you adopt that before this downturn?

Peter Jueptner: We changed that in the downturn. We said, "You know, it's impossible to predict."

Rik Geiersbach: What's interesting for me is talking about the indisputables. I think if you had asked me a year ago what issues would be challenged today, I wouldn't have guessed the ones that I'm working with now.

On the defense side, we have shifting national budget priorities, which are putting pressure on our national security spend. I don't think I would have anticipated that. I thought that the defense spend would go with the threat environment. That's the way we always operated. But now there's a crowding out on the defense side.

On the commercial side, we're seeing emerging new competitors, which I probably wouldn't have gauged as coming online as fast as I think they will now, due to new economic nationalism that's changing global trade rules.

Niki Manby: Do you think that nationalism fuels or stalls innovation?

Rik Geiersbach: I think in many ways it could be a catalyst for us on the product-development side, knowing that there's emerging new competitors—be they China or Russia or Japan—which are probably going to come on line sooner than anticipated. On the other hand, a global trade dispute over any of these issues could get difficult for everybody.

Peter Jueptner: That triggers a thought. I think there's definitely a new normal in terms of the flexibility you need to have in running the business. And I think that's going to stay. Adaptability is front and center. The time when you could just count on the market growing 5 to 7 percent a year on the same trajectory is over for quite some time, I think. You will see distortions in the system and different trends emerging.

The _Quarterly_: _How does that need for greater flexibility play out in how you run the company?_

To watch a video of the full conversation, visit mckinseyquarterly.com.

Peter Jueptner: We basically have an ongoing strategy discussion and a quarterly budget discussion: looking ahead for the year, discussing what to do, and reallocating resources. So it's much shorter term in terms of how you do your resource allocation. Usually you do your budget and then you don't change much over the course of the year. Now we're basically changing and adjusting quarterly.

Peter Pintar: We did three presentations to our board with our annual budget, and probably had four revisions on what our industry outlook was, even just for the current year. The industry downcycle has been much more severe than what we had anticipated even just months ago.

Niki Manby: The word that I think we have to pair with *flexibility* is *alignment*. You want to be nimble, but at the same time you want to make sure you're turning whole ships, not just parts.

So we think a lot about the fact that strategy should drive structure and structure should drive processes. If you are making changes in one, how do you ensure the company is making changes to the other? How do you make sure your corporate processes and the structure that you've got in place are actually in line with where you want to go strategically? Inherent in these changes is instituting more of an ongoing planning process. It's easy to say that. But it's very difficult to engage employees to always be thinking about how to react and create processes that allow the organization to respond and make decisions in a continuous way.

Rik Geiersbach: One thing we've been very deliberate about this year, which I think has been moderately successful, is instituting "potential" reviews—do the underlying assumptions that you baked into your plan still hold? You can do those periodically throughout your organization, rather than just doing the annual cycles.

Peter Jueptner: I think the point Niki made around the alignment of the leadership in the company is critically important. Making sure that you break down the silos and have those discussions is the only way to really do this. That requires more parallel processing. I think we're sort of done with the sequential way.

The *Quarterly*: *You're all talking about a faster planning cycle— not annually, but quarterly, or even continuously. It takes a lot of time for people to do that. So what are you* not *doing? What are you cutting out of your planning process as you compress the cycle time?*

Niki Manby: One of the things that we're doing is thinking about target setting for business units a little differently, and incorporating a cushion, for lack of a better word, so that you can think about funding new opportunities outside of the annual planning process. If you don't have a process that allows you to execute on pillars of your strategy throughout the year, you're probably missing some opportunities. To suggest that transformational growth opportunities are identified, fully baked, and ready for a proposal and blessing in the same month every year is obviously not realistic in our environment. So we have a planning process and, frankly, a budget methodology that allows for retaining investment funds of significant enough scale that you can seize opportunities as they become real throughout the year. I also think it will have a silver-lining effect of reducing the pressure that comes in the annual planning process.

Rik Geiersbach: I'm not sure I've given much thought to what we've given up, given the increased pace in the strategic-planning cycle. But one thing we've been thoughtful about is trying to take the

strategy function—which is now enjoying an increased relevance— and wall it off, saying, "Look, our job is to be the long-term health advocates for the enterprise. There're an army of folks making sure that planes fly and satellites get launched. Our responsibility is to be looking over the horizon."

Peter Jueptner: That's a good point. A danger in this whole thing is that strategy becomes too operational. I think this has happened a bit over the past year because everything became more short term. That's one of the things I'm worried about. We may not put as much emphasis on the really long term, because there's not a whole lot of time for it right now. And it's actually more important than ever.

Rik Geiersbach: I agree. You have to remove yourself from the day-to-day trench warfare and tell the chairman or others, "That's actually not even the hill that we want to take. We want to take the hill over there."

Niki Manby: Do you think that your definition of *long* has changed as you think about that long-range planning?

Peter Jueptner: We're still doing a three- to five-year outlook. We're not intending to change that. I think we still need a backbone, longer-term outlook with shorter-term flexibility.

The *Quarterly*: *Any final thoughts?*

Peter Pintar: Companies are coming into this recession with very different balance sheets. Some companies have billions of dollars of cash, others 50 percent leverage. In that environment, the range of options for the players is very, very different. It's not clear what the constellation of competition is going to look like in a few years. But I'm certain it's going to be shaped by what's going on right now, with the stretched companies getting acquired, splitting up, or going under—and the cash-rich companies looking for ways to deploy those resources, recognizing that this may be in fact a very unique opportunity to pick up assets or invest in growth.

So I think that, competitively, the structure of who the players are and how they're aligned and who's better off relative to somebody else is going to be very different in a few years. I'm not sure it's that different from other industry cycles, but because this downturn has been so severe, the opportunity is much more profound.

Peter Jueptner: It's a key point. You know, we've seen very little M&A activity over the last one-and-a-half years—across industries. My expectation would be, in our industry, we're going to see M&A activity picking up significantly over the next 12 months. There will be more of a shakeout and a rearranging of players. o

Related articles on mckinseyquarterly.com

Strategic planning: Three tips for 2009

How chief strategy officers think about their role: A roundtable

Strategy in a 'structural break'

We welcome your comments on this article. Please send them to quarterly_comments@mckinsey.com.

By Invitation: Insights and opinion from outside contributors

Competing through organizational agility

Three distinct types of agility—strategic, portfolio, and operational—help companies navigate turbulence. Each of them has its own sources and challenges.

Donald Sull

Market turbulence did not begin with the fall of Lehman Brothers, and it will not end when the global economy recovers.[1] Indeed, a variety of academic studies—using measures such as stock price volatility, the mortality of firms, the persistence of superior performance, the frequency of economic shocks, and the speed of technology dissemination—have concluded that volatility at the firm level increased somewhere between two- and fourfold from the 1970s to the 1990s (see sidebar, "Recommended reading").

In turbulent markets, organizational agility, which I define as the capacity to identify and capture opportunities more quickly than rivals do, is invaluable. Executives know this: a recent McKinsey survey found that nine out of ten executives ranked organizational agility both as critical to business success and as growing in importance over time.[2] The benefits of enhanced agility, according to survey respondents, include higher revenues, more satisfied customers and employees, improved operational efficiency, and a faster time to market.

Over the past decade, I have analyzed more and less successful companies in some of the world's most turbulent geographical and

Don Sull is a professor of management practice at the London Business School and author of *The Upside of Turbulence*, which introduced the concept of operational, portfolio, and strategic agility.

[1] I define turbulence as a measure of the frequency of unpredictable changes affecting the ability of companies to create and sustain value.
[2] "Building a nimble organization: A McKinsey Global Survey," mckinseyquarterly.com, July 2006.

product markets, including China, Brazil, European fast fashion, and financial services. This research underscores the importance of agility for success in turbulent markets. My findings also revealed three distinct types of agility: strategic, portfolio, and operational. Strategic agility consists of spotting and seizing game-changing opportunities. Portfolio agility is the capacity to shift resources—including cash, talent, and managerial attention—quickly and effectively out of less promising business areas and into more attractive ones. And operational agility involves exploiting opportunities within a focused business model.

Many organizations rely on a single form of agility—companies like Southwest Airlines or Tesco excel at seizing operational opportunities, while private-equity groups like TPG Capital or Kohlberg Kravis & Roberts (KKR) succeed through active portfolio management. In turbulent markets, however, overreliance on a single type of agility can be dangerous. An operationally agile company, for example, is at risk if its core business becomes less attractive. By detailing how companies have enhanced each type of agility, this article seeks to help other managers do the same.

Recommended reading

The works below present evidence on rising market turbulence, which can be measured in a number of ways:

Firm-level volatility
Diego A. Comin and Thomas Philippon, "The rise in firm-level volatility: Causes and consequences," *NBER Macroeconomics Annual*, 2005, Volume 20, pp. 167–228.

Probability of exit
George P. Baker and Robert E. Kennedy, "Survivorship and the economic grim reaper," *Journal of Law, Economics, and Organization*, 2002, Volume 18, Number 2, pp. 324–61.

The speed with which industry leaders fall from their thrones
William I. Huyett and S. Patrick Viguerie, "Extreme competition," mckinseyquarterly.com, February 2005.

Robert R. Wiggins and Timothy W. Ruefli, "Schumpeter's ghost: Is hyper competition making the best of times shorter?" *Strategic Management Journal*, 2005, Volume 26, Number 10, pp. 887–911.

Strategic agility

Many complex interactive systems—such as weather patterns, seismic activity, and traffic—follow what mathematicians call an inverse power law: the frequency of an event is inversely related to its magnitude. In turbulent markets, an inverse power law implies that companies face a steady flow of small opportunities, periodic midsize ones, and the rare chance to create significant value. Examples of golden opportunities include major acquisitions, transformational mergers, the opening of booming markets such as China or India, launching a breakthrough product like the iPhone, or securing hard assets on favorable terms during an economic crisis.

Given the unpredictable nature and uneven distribution of golden opportunities, a combination of patience (to wait for the right time to strike) and boldness (acting when that time arises) is crucial. Carnival, for example, entered the cruise business in 1972 but didn't build any new ships until the late 1970s, when CEO Ted Arison recognized that airline deregulation would reduce the price of flying to Miami just as the television series *The Love Boat* was serendipitously educating consumers on the merits of cruises. As Carnival commissioned the industry's first new ship in nearly a decade, the industry leader, Royal Caribbean, enlarged two existing ships by carving them in half with welding torches and inserting a new midsection. By the time Royal Caribbean ordered new ships, Carnival had seized a large chunk of the growing market.

An effective combination of patience and boldness is easy to recognize in hindsight. But pulling it off in the heat of battle is no mean feat. Observing a sizable number of organizations that have demonstrated strategic agility has highlighted for me three principles that may prove useful for other companies.

Probing for opportunities

In recent decades, few companies have demonstrated more strategic agility than Spain's Banco Santander, which rose from a midsize Spanish bank in the 1980s to become one of the world's ten most valuable banks today. Santander built a strong presence in Latin America when the opportunity presented itself and snapped up two UK banks, Alliance & Leicester and Bradford & Bingley, during the current economic crisis.

Santander's approach illustrates the value of small-scale probes to help companies explore potential opportunities. In the late 1980s, Santander explored other European markets, the United States, and Latin America through small acquisitions, minority stakes, and alliances. Some of these probes paid off, others didn't, but collectively they exposed Santander to diverse opportunity streams. When currency crises roiled Latin America's markets in the late 1990s, Santander seized the moment, making a series of investments to build the region's largest banking franchise. While waiting for golden opportunities to emerge, Santander executives introduced a series of new products while improving operations and risk management.

In the current environment, many start-ups and established companies need funds to bolster their balance sheets. Established companies can invest modest amounts of cash—in the form of minority stakes or participation in joint ventures—to buy access to information on future opportunities.

Mitigating risk

Some managers cloak recklessness under the mantle of strategic agility. The most effective leaders, however, systematically minimize the downside risk of upside bets. Consider the example of Mittal Steel (now ArcelorMittal), which rose from a single minimill in Indonesia to global leadership through a series of acquisitions in some of the world's most volatile markets.

Mittal actively managed risks by screening potential acquisitions for access to growth markets, low-cost labor, energy, and raw materials to boost the odds of future profitability. The company avoided overpaying, instead buying money-losing mills from government owners in Trinidad and Mexico for about 10 percent of their construction cost, while convincing the governments to finance most of the purchase price. The company's due-diligence teams consisted of operating executives from other Mittal plants, who would be responsible for integrating the plant if acquired—an approach that ensured a realistic assessment of its potential and an actionable integration plan.

It is a buyer's market for many assets right now. Companies should not only haggle over price but also, like Mittal, negotiate hard on nonprice deal terms in order to surface and mitigate possible risks.

Staying in the game

Sometimes, the key is simply staying in the game until a big chance emerges. Apple's launch of the iPod and move into the digital music business is, rightly, the stock example of game-changing strategic agility. But it was Apple's ability to stay in the game long enough to wait for the opportunity to arise that made the difference. During the 1990s, Apple's share of the personal-computer market fell below 5 percent, relegating the company's products to the "other" category, while its stock price was flat from the late 1980s through early 2004. Loyal customers and a strong brand allowed Apple to wait for new contextual circumstances to generate a golden opportunity.

> An effective combination of patience and boldness is easy to recognize in hindsight—but pulling it off in the heat of battle is no mean feat

Many managers equate staying in the game with a strong balance sheet. A war chest of cash, however, is only one of several structural attributes that allow a company to weather changes in the market and live to fight another day. Other attributes include sheer size; diversification of cash flows; customer lock-in; low fixed costs; rare resources, such as brands, expertise, or hard assets that customers will pay for; and a powerful patron, such as a regulator, investor, or customer with a vested interest in a company's success.

An environment like the one we've been experiencing, where cash is scarce, represents an opportune moment for executives to inventory all of their companies' sources of resilience and to develop a plan to stay in the game. The plan might include actions such as lobbying for trade finance from the government or taking steps to decrease fixed costs as a hedge against future price or volume reductions.

Portfolio agility

A set of common pathologies often gets in the way when companies with diverse business portfolios try to shift resources out of less promising areas and into more promising ones. Resource allocation in most large, complex organizations follows a bottom-up trajectory: frontline employees spot opportunities, middle managers lend their support to promising projects, and senior executives rubber-stamp proposals from trusted subordinates. This process stalls in reverse, however, and fails to foster disinvestment, since managers rarely recommend killing projects that might damage their reputations or endanger the livelihoods of their subordinates.

Portfolio agility can also break down when managers apply a uniform set of objectives, such as a fixed gross-margin percentage or time-to-break-even, across all opportunities, regardless of their stage or long-term potential. And portfolios grow stale when executives grip the reins of power for too long, blocking up-and-coming managers from leadership positions and sticking to traditional businesses because that is what the veterans know best. Facing difficult portfolio choices, seasoned executives may err on the side of loss aversion by protecting established businesses (which they often built and ran) while avoiding risky bets on the future. For example, the late Reginald H. Jones, Jack Welch's predecessor at GE, shied away from some difficult decisions, such as exiting the Utah International mining-company deal, which he himself had pushed.

Many companies think that developing disciplined processes for evaluating individual business units will ensure portfolio agility. This is incorrect. Reginald Jones had the formal tools to classify the company's strategic business units but still failed to make some hard calls. Portfolio agility requires managers to base these decisions on logic and data rather than emotion and politics and to have the courage to implement unpopular decisions. When Jack Welch became CEO, he reversed many of his predecessor's missteps, pruning GE's portfolio in his early years on the job. More impressive still, Welch also reversed his own mistakes. For example, when Welch's Kidder, Peabody acquisition failed to meet expectations, he first fired the head of the business—an old friend—and ultimately sold the company. Simultaneously, Welch oversaw a massive investment in GE Capital, even though he did not always see eye-to-eye with its leadership.

Top executives also need the power to control and allocate key resources at the group rather than business unit level. One large North American bank conducted a major study to profile its diverse business units in painstaking detail and made a compelling argument to shift cash, management talent, and IT resources from two established businesses into promising new ones. The bank, however, was a

Watch a video interview with Don Sull, in which he discusses his book *The Upside of Turbulence*, on mckinseyquarterly.com.

loose federation of units, and the group CEO lacked the power or precedent to reallocate resources across fiefdoms. The cash cows continued to hoard their resources while the promising businesses withered for lack of funds.

To enhance portfolio agility, companies must reallocate not only cash but also people. Before doing so, they should cultivate a cadre of general managers versatile enough to move from business to business. Companies such as HSBC and Mars invest heavily to develop general managers by giving them P&L responsibility early on, rotating them through functions and markets, and offering leadership training. As a result, such companies can redeploy their managers to emerging opportunities, even if they do not know in advance what form those opportunities might take.

During a boom, managers tend to spread resources evenly—like peanut butter on bread—to maximize perceived fairness and minimize conflict. In a downturn, they should avoid the temptation to spread the pain evenly across all units and instead disinvest from less promising operations to free resources for more promising ones. They can also use the current crisis to renew their processes for making portfolio decisions. Many executives centralize resource allocation in a crisis. Rather than decentralizing when the economy picks up again, senior executives can institutionalize processes to reallocate management talent and cash across units in order to preserve portfolio agility in the future.

Operational agility

An organization's ability to exploit both revenue-enhancing and cost-cutting opportunities within its core business more quickly, effectively, and consistently than rivals do is the source of operational ability. Managers cannot predict the form, magnitude, or timing of these opportunities in advance. They can, however, boost the odds of beating their rivals to them. While there are a number of important steps executives hoping to build operational agility can take, I focus here on two: putting in place systems to gather and share the information required to spot opportunities and building processes to translate corporate priorities into focused action.

Data to spot opportunities

Over the past few years, the Spanish retailer Zara, which overtook Gap in 2008 as the world's largest clothing retailer, has been a poster child for supply chain excellence because of its ability to deliver new items to stores quickly. Impressive as this supply chain is, the retailer's ability to spot trends as they emerge is equally important in serving its target customers—fashion-conscious young women in Europe. Zara consistently spots these opportunities because it has built-in systems to collect real-time market data, to supplement statistical reports with periodic exposure to raw market data, and to share information widely throughout the organization.

Zara's cross-functional design teams pore over daily sales and inventory reports to see what is selling and what is not, and they continually update their view of the market. Twice-weekly orders from store managers provide further real-time information on what might sell. Zara managers supplement these quantitative reports with regular visits to the field to collect firsthand data that standardized reports miss. In the summer of 2007, for instance, Zara introduced a line of slim-fit clothes, including "pencil" skirts in bright colors. Daily sales statistics revealed that the items were not selling but shed no light on why. Zara marketing managers visited the stores to explore the situation in person and learned that women loved how the slim-fit clothes looked but couldn't fit into their usual sizes when they tried on the garments. Armed with this insight, Zara recalled the items and replaced the labels with the next sizes down. Sales exploded.

To ensure that the data are widely shared, Zara locates designers, marketing managers, and buyers in the company's La Coruña headquarters, where they work in open-plan offices. Frequent discussions, serendipitous encounters, and visual inspection help teams diagnose the overall market situation, see how their work fits into the big picture, and spot opportunities that might otherwise fall between the cracks of organizational silos.

Recently, many companies have increased the frequency of their strategic and operational reviews and drawn, ad hoc, on different sources of data in order to understand the broader market context. They should not let these practices lapse as the economy recovers. Rather, companies ought to institutionalize the collection of real-time data, supplement these with periodic firsthand observations in the field, and disseminate information widely throughout the organization.

Translating corporate priorities into individual objectives

In many companies, agility stalls in the boardroom when top executives deluge the organization with multiple and often conflicting priorities. That's not the case at Banco Garantia and its affiliated companies, including the retailer Lojas Americanas, the logistics company América Latina Logistica, and, formerly, the brewer AmBev (which merged with Interbrew in 2004 and acquired Anheuser-Busch in 2008, creating Anheuser-Busch InBev). Garantia's companies operate in Brazil, traditionally one of the world's most turbulent markets, and have succeeded through operational agility.

Garantia companies avoid the proliferation of corporate priorities by capping their number at three to five in any year. Executives communicate them clearly throughout the organization to focus attention, resources, and effort on a handful of "must win" battles. Then managers translate corporate priorities into individual objectives. Subordinates negotiate with their bosses to set three to five individual objectives, when possible favoring quantitative targets and those that can be measured on an ongoing basis.

Related articles on mckinseyquarterly.com

The 21st-century organization

Building a nimble organization: A McKinsey Global Survey

Just-in-time strategy for a turbulent world

To maintain focus on individual objectives, managers in each Garantia company work in an open office, with their individual objectives hanging behind their desks for all to see. A red, yellow, or green dot denotes progress on each objective. To ensure that individual objectives are aligned with one another and with overarching priorities, the CEO of America Latina Logistica spends one weekend each year reviewing performance targets for his top 200 executives, flagging inconsistencies and questions.

A downturn brings hard choices into stark relief, provides an external rationale to justify difficult decisions, and offers "air cover" with external stakeholders (including investors and directors) to reverse previous decisions. In the current market, senior executives should consolidate their major initiatives into a single list and make the hard choices needed to select a handful that are truly critical. To ensure that everyone gets the message, they should communicate the priorities throughout the entire organization, along with a list of initiatives that are no longer key objectives, to ensure that people do not waste resources on unimportant matters.

One final thought: economic crises can provide an ideal opportunity to invigorate the cultural transformation that is often needed to cultivate operational agility. For example, in the transition from good South Korean player to great global company, Samsung Electronics made most of its progress during the global recession of the early 1990s and the "Asian contagion" of 1997. Senior executives used these crises to renew a sense of urgency, justify unpopular decisions, and overcome complacency or resistance to change. Focusing on culture is critical because outexecuting rivals time and time again requires constant injections of urgency, effort, and enthusiasm.[3] A performance-oriented culture helps induce such effort.

• • •

Traditionally, managers have been equated with ship captains, peering through a telescope deep into the future, setting a long-term vision, and proceeding steady as she goes. In the new normal, however, managers must proceed through an impenetrable fog that obscures any view of the future. By building the organization's strategic, portfolio, and operational agility, managers can position their companies to succeed, come what may. O

[3] The importance of values and a performance culture to operational agility is a broader topic than space allows me to treat fully here. Chapter nine of my book *The Upside of Turbulence* (HarperBusiness, 2009) addresses the issue in more detail.

A CEO's guide to reenergizing the senior team

In today's tough and fast-changing environment, CEOs must help their top leaders to work through fear and denial and to learn new rules.

Derek Dean

When business conditions change as dramatically as they have in the past year, CEOs need to be able to rely on their best leaders to adapt quickly. But what should they do when their strongest executives seem unable to play a new game? The costs—organizational drift, missed opportunities, unaddressed threats—are so big that it's tempting to replace leaders who are suffering from paralysis. But this is a mistake when, as is often the case, these executives possess valuable assets, such as superior market knowledge, relationships, and organizational savvy, that are difficult to replace.

Before sending promising executives off the field, CEOs should try to help them learn to play by new rules. While part of the task—making a compelling case for change, helping him or her meet new job demands—involves appealing to an executive's rational side, there's also frequently an emotional element that is at least as important. Empathizing with the complex emotions executives may be feeling as the assumptions underlying their business approach unravel can be a critical part of overcoming the fear, denial, and learning blocks keeping them stuck.

Helping senior managers swim through this thick stew of challenges is a perennial problem that has become more acute for many organizations over the last year (see sidebar, "CEOs, tough times, and emotions"). The credit crunch and global economic slowdown didn't

Derek Dean is a director in McKinsey's San Francisco office.

just cause the unraveling of many business models. They also unsettled the assumptions and confidence of many senior managers. Mopping up the collateral damage in the executive suite is now a mission-critical task for many CEOs and is likely to remain one even when business conditions begin to recover.

Overcoming fear

Among the many emotions that can influence how executives interpret and respond to events, there's one worth addressing on its own: plain old white-knuckled fear. In times of rapid change, when the actions that used to lead to success don't any more, even strong leaders can experience intense, unproductive levels of fear caused by threats to their identity, their reputations, their social standing, and even their basic survival needs of a job and a paycheck. Ironically, leaders with the strongest track records are often *more* susceptible to fear during tumultuous periods because they have less experience facing adversity than their colleagues with more checkered pasts do.

Spiking levels of fear can convert frank, flexible, open, and self-reflective leaders into defensive, close-minded, rigid, and literal ones. These leaders may take things personally, feel persecuted, cease productive self-reflection, and lose the ability to process new infor-

CEOs, tough times, and emotions

Robert I. Sutton

Derek Dean's piece echoes numerous recent conversations I've had with CEOs who tell me they are spending big hunks of time helping top-team members who are 'freaking out.' It also is right in line with academic research indicating that anxiety, cognitive narrowing, and clinging tightly to old ways are natural responses when individuals and groups feel overwhelmed by scary events that they did not anticipate, do not understand, and believe they cannot control.

Here I want to expand on Mr. Dean's argument in three ways. One is to underscore a point that's implicit but unstated in his essay: CEOs must work just as doggedly to confront and deal with their own demons and foibles as they do to help their charges come to grips with theirs. This is crucial because followers—who usually watch the boss's moves closely anyway—become hyperfocused on every little move that their superiors make when they are worried about what tough financial times will mean for their fates.

An executive in a leadership program at Stanford, for example, described an assistant in his office who stopped a senior executive in the hall to ask him, 'When are the layoffs coming?' This executive was dumbfounded by the question because, though layoffs were in the works, this was a well-guarded secret. After the executive confessed that job cuts were likely to happen, he asked how she knew. She explained that he had been unable to look anyone in the eye all day and instead looked down at his shoes when he spoke to others. She further said it was well known that when this boss was 'having an interesting shoes day,' it meant that bad news was on the way. The lesson is that executives, including CEOs, are real people too. Especially during tough times, they must go to even greater efforts than usual to unearth the fears that they can't quite articulate or don't feel safe enough to reveal. And they must make it safe enough for their people to point out when they are spreading fear or clinging irrationally to misguided assumptions.[1]

Robert Sutton is a professor of management science and engineering at Stanford University. His upcoming book, *Good Boss, Bad Boss*, will be published by Business Plus in 2010.

mation and respond to difficult situations. Others in the organization will notice this, of course, and will let the executive know in subtle ways—reinforcing fear and defensiveness.

Breaking this cycle doesn't require a CEO to become an armchair psychotherapist, but it does require engaging team members on an emotional level. As leadership-development expert Donald Novak puts it, "Helping executives verbalize their emotions and acknowledge their validity can allow them to move past fear and become more productive." Putting fear on the table, so to speak, helps get it out of the way.

To understand what this kind of empathetic coaching looks like in practice, consider the CEO of a large global firm who recently discovered that one of his best functional executives had become "stuck." Although this executive, at the outset of the downturn, had led his peers in dialing back investment and then cutting costs, he had subsequently boxed himself into a corner, telling the CEO, "I simply cannot cut any more if you still expect me to support the business." The CEO addressed this paralysis in a conversation about his functional leader's underlying fears: of failure, of disappointing his boss, and of losing his team, to name just a few. The CEO admitted that he had some of the same fears and emphasized that this was a completely

---

The second thing that struck me was how well Harrah's Entertainment CEO Gary Loveman seemed to understand that when senior teams are freaked out and frozen in their tracks, the only way to enable reasonable decision making is to create a psychological safety zone. My research and experience suggest that CEOs create safety through the hundreds of little things that they say and do when dealing with their teams—like smiling at the right time, offering praise and reassurance, admitting their own mistakes, and gently but firmly calling out people who fuel fear, cynicism, and hostility. This is why being a skilled leader, especially a CEO, requires years of experience and relentless attention to tiny details, and why the job is a lot harder than it looks.

Finally, I would use the term 'small-wins strategy' to describe Gary Loveman's encouragement of efforts aimed at rapidly identifying and implementing a host of small steps to reduce services and amenities in ways that do not alienate customers. As University of Michigan professor Karl Weick has shown, when people frame problems as enormous and insurmountable challenges, this drives up their anxiety and causes them to feel helpless: the problem seems so big that there is nothing they can do to make progress. They therefore freak out and freeze in their tracks. Breaking down a problem into bite-sized pieces (what Weick calls small wins) calms people and helps them take constructive action.[2] This strategy is especially useful during tough times, as it both dampens fears and gives people a much-needed feeling of control—and enables them to make collective progress in the right direction.

[1] To see more on "interesting shoes days" and other ways the spotlight increases on managers in difficult times, watch "Good boss, bad times," our May 2009 interview with Bob Sutton, available on mckinseyquarterly.com.

[2] For more on how leaders can employ the small-wins approach, see Bob Sutton, "How to be a good boss in a bad economy," *Harvard Business Review*, 2009, Volume 87, Number 6, pp. 42–50.

normal way to react. This acknowledgement helped the executive
out of his corner and stirred a discussion about ways to reinvent the
function without sacrificing performance.

When CEOs acknowledge their own fears, they strip away the stigma
attached to the emotion and make it easier for other executives to
move beyond it. It's also important for CEOs to examine the role that
they play in reinforcing fears. They may need to change some kinds
of behavior (such as blustering about the consequences of underperfor-
mance) in order to engage productively with their team. They may
need to address anxiety about reputations and job security more trans-
parently than usual. Finally, the CEO needs to model the "right" sort
of behavior, including openness to dialgue and collaboration, respect
for all opinions, and self-confidence.

Overcoming denial

In addition to the impact that fear has on how people interpret events,
cognitive errors can lead even the most talented executives to deny
otherwise clear evidence that times have really changed. Until recently,
for example, several key members of a global semiconductor company's senior team were reporting to their CEO that the present downturn was little different from other recessions they had experienced
throughout their careers in this highly cyclical industry. A revenue drop
of more than 50 percent over two quarters didn't change their con-
viction. Some of their comments to the CEO could populate a textbook
list of cognitive errors underlying denial:

"We just got an order last week, so things are turning"
    —a classic example of the availability heuristic

"This feels just like the last downturn; we'll come back eventually"
    —an anchoring error

"My team agrees this will resolve itself"
    —the bandwagon effect

*"I found three different studies that support my view that this is
a temporary downturn"*
    —the confirmation bias

"We need to study this more before we act irrationally"
    —the information bias

"If we do the things we usually do in a downturn, everything will be OK"
    —the optimism bias

To combat these symptoms of denial, the CEO sought to overwhelm his
team with objective data and analysis: the conditions facing the
company's customers and end consumers across a variety of economic
sectors around the world. Through a series of exhausting working
sessions, he immersed the entire team in raw data and used peer pressure to keep the team honest and expose cognitive biases early.
In many cases, he needed to hold separate one-on-one meetings to

help his top managers understand and emotionally process the full implications of market changes—including the improbability that several businesses would ever recover to historical levels.

It took about a month, but in the end the CEO successfully overcame the denial he had originally faced from his team. Once grounded in the new reality, his best executives began leading serious reassessments of their strategies. Many had to reevaluate their product portfolios from the ground up, change their sales and marketing approaches, and eliminate activities and functions that used to be core to their strategies. Like true converts, they became zealous in rooting out any biases and denial they encountered among their teams.

Overcoming learning blocks

Provoking members of the top team to confront their fears and embrace the need for change is an important starting point, but it still leaves an enormous task before the CEO: helping the team learn new ways of doing business in response to changing conditions. When Harrah's Entertainment CEO Gary Loveman talks about the difficulty successful executives face in learning, he likes to quote a line from a 1991 *Harvard Business Review* article by Chris Argyris: "Because many professionals are almost always successful at what they do, they rarely experience failure. And because they have rarely failed, they have never learned how to learn from failure."[1]

Yet failure, or at least the dramatic upending of what yields success, is exactly what many executives face during times of tumultuous change. The basis of their success—clear mandates and time horizons, experience-based judgment, the ability to convert data into useful information for decision making, and a clear understanding of cultural norms—can go out the window overnight. Serious upheaval means mandates can become ambiguous and highly dynamic. Time horizons may shrink dramatically, forcing executives into a near-constant scramble to replan and redesign their strategies as the ground shifts beneath them. And time-tested approaches, such as careful analysis and consensus building, can bog things down—a serious problem when the biggest risk may be not changing quickly enough.

At Harrah's, Loveman was confronted with the need to help his top team relearn how to succeed when the company experienced its first real revenue decline while striving to meet the debt service demands of its 2008 leveraged buyout. For years, Harrah's had expanded revenue and earnings consistently through a combination of customer relationship marketing, tailored guest service, and an incredibly strong loyalty program. The recession challenged the way Harrah's applied these tools to generate sales growth at each gaming location.

[1] Chris Argyris, "Teaching smart people how to learn," *Harvard Business Review*, 1991, Volume 69, Number 3, pp. 99–109.

And as things turned out, "the right actions in times of retrenchment," said Loveman, were "not the symmetrical opposite of the right actions during growth." The result of this asymmetry was a change in the job demands for nearly every member of his senior team.

To help his leaders learn, Loveman followed many of the approaches described earlier: acknowledging his team's emotions and immersing those teams in raw data and analysis. But more than that, Loveman pushed the members of his senior team to reexamine the fundamental "truths" upon which they had built successful businesses and careers. He challenged them to lay out the assumptions behind their past successes, and if those assumptions no longer held he charged them to go beyond simply adjusting their business and analytic models by running them down instead of up. Rather, in many cases, it was necessary to build completely new models.

Related articles on mckinseyquarterly.com

The CEO's role in leading transformation

The psychology of change management

Corporate transformation under pressure

For example, Harrah's had for years faced highly elastic demand curves with its core gaming customers: offering them incentives and rewards stimulated incremental visits and revenue (both gaming and nongaming). In this recession, Harrah's found itself confronted with inelastic demand curves in several of its key segments. As a result, it seemed impossible to justify the company's traditional types of marketing investments; they simply couldn't stimulate the customer behavior (and associated revenue) needed to generate positive returns.

One result was that Harrah's needed to cut its costs dramatically, which involved figuring out ways to reduce services, amenities, staffing levels, and "comps" without angering loyal customers. But the trickier challenge has been to learn new ways of applying the old tools (relationship marketing, guest service, and loyalty programs) in response to new and different customer behavior. The learning process instigated by Loveman has helped Harrah's leaders create new rules to manage falling as well as rising investments, to stimulate growth with less capital, and to deliver guest service effectively at much lower cost. These new rules, in turn, have led to new job mandates, new data to manage the business, and new norms for decision making—norms the team has put into action through a series of marketing, service, and lean-operations pilots.

Fear, denial, and the need to learn aren't new challenges, but more senior executives are falling prey to them in today's shockingly tough and fast-changing environment. It's up to CEOs to help their leaders work through these issues, including the powerful emotions involved. o

Letters to the Editor

Reader comments on "A CEO's guide to reenergizing the senior team" from mckinseyquarterly.com.

I work with CEOs and see people suffering from "white knuckle fear" who are able to express it. What I do not see enough of is their direct reports feeling the freedom to express themselves, and this creates paralysis in the organization at a crucial level.

Alison Bond
Director, *The Halo Works*
Surrey, UK

A good article and informative for CEOs. However, its basic premise is that CEOs know better and can guide the executives. This is usually not the case. It would be better if "board of directors" was substituted in place of "CEO."

Fakhruddin Ahmed
Head of international payments and banking relationships,
Islamic Development Bank
Jeddah, Saudi Arabia

This article is not just for CEOs but for every senior and executive manager. My experience with C-levels is that they are usually too busy to free up time to work closely with their direct reports to build trust and confidence, and to empower them to drive necessary change.

Tobias Kuners of Koenders
Director, *Wolters Kluwer Pharma Solutions*
Amsterdam, Netherlands

Recalibrating expectations is equally key to help the team learn how to play the game with the changed rules.

Ashok Kapoor
Group director, HR, Asia-Pacific,
Black & Decker
Shanghai, China

Tells you more and more how humility—the necessary condition for any of the above solutions to work—is in such short supply.

Mahadevan Sundarraj
Director and principal consultant,
Collabrant Incubators
Bangalore, India

Thank you for stating what is often left unsaid about executives: like every other human being, they are driven by their emotions. To state otherwise is another form of denial.

Ro Gorell
Managing director,
Ascent2change
Berkshire, UK

Visit mckinseyquarterly.com for more reader responses to this and other articles.

Center Stage

A look at current trends and topics in management

A better way to cut costs

Suzanne Heywood, Dennis Layton, and Risto Penttinen

Suzanne Heywood
is a principal in
McKinsey's London
office, where **Dennis
Layton** is an associate
principal; **Risto
Penttinen** is a principal
in the Helsinki office.

According to a recent *McKinsey Quarterly* survey, 79 percent of all companies have cut costs in response to the global economic crisis—but only 53 percent of executives think that doing so has helped their companies to weather it.

One reason for this disconnect: in an effort to make cuts seem more straightforward and fair, companies tend to cut about equally everywhere—without considering their strategic needs. A second issue, with longer-term consequences, is that quick head count reductions often come at a price—missing the opportunities that crises can create to improve business systems or to strengthen parts of an organization selectively.

Our experience suggests that companies can cut costs in a better way. They should begin any initiative by thinking through whether they could restructure the business to take advantage of current and projected marketplace trends (for instance, by exiting relatively low-profit or low-growth businesses) or to mitigate threats, such as consolidating competitors. An important part of the analysis is to understand a company's financial situation and the range of potential outcomes under a number of different external economic scenarios. Second, within the resulting strategy, take time to understand which activities drive value and which activities do or could make the organization competitively distinctive. Organizations should invest in value-creating activities and cut costs in others while meeting clear financial goals in a set time frame. **O**

The full version of this article is available on mckinseyquarterly.com.

Lloyd Miller

Exploring three sources of value

Senior executives should ensure that cost-cutting efforts reflect a company's strategy. Here are three ways to do so.

Restructuring to reflect your future

1

Restructuring to reflect your future. When considering each of these areas, think about the right structure, given the strategy, to pursue in the most probable future; what structural changes to make regardless of the future; and specific events that would trigger structural moves.

- Reconsider the core business model and focus; whether to enter or leave businesses, geographies, or joint ventures; and vertical integration.
- Rethink organizational design, including the relationships among the corporate center and the business units.
- Resolve unfinished business, such as incomplete merger integration.

Cutting the fat

2

To determine which of these potential actions will be most effective, create an accurate cost baseline, with details at the regional and business unit level, and assess the value of potential costs against that baseline. Set priorities by assessing each action's potential value and ease of implementation.

- Remove layers from the organization and expand managers' span of control.
- Eliminate redundant or irrelevant functions, processes, or activities.
- Apply lean techniques to repeatable or low-value activities.
- Reconsider the role of the corporate center.
- Consolidate activities to gain scale, scope, or knowledge.
- Clarify roles across the company to create accountability; reset pay grades.
- Enforce high-productivity standards.

Building capabilities

3

To determine which capabilities to focus on, quantitatively assess the potential gain from improving them and qualitatively assess the value of greater organizational effectiveness.

- Identify where the organization is now weak—perhaps because complexity is slowing action, the right people aren't in the right places, pivotal roles are weak, performance scorecards for the business or employees are ineffective, or leaders don't have time to focus on critical tasks.
- Determine where stronger capabilities—in functions such as IT, finance, or sales or in specific activities—could help.

Special report:

The water imperative

Businesses and governments the world over are feeling the impact of water scarcity. As populations and economies continue to grow, the demand for water will rise as well, leaving a majority constrained by limited resources and inefficient policies.

These articles examine the economics of water management, the technologies available to increase water productivity, and how companies can seize the opportunity in the market for water conservation.

The Aral Sea, drained to a fraction of its size by irrigation canals that tap into the lake's feeder rivers.   © Gerd Ludwig/Corbis

The business opportunity in water conservation

For many companies, water efficiency is a long-term requirement for staying in business, a big commercial opportunity, or both.

Giulio Boccaletti, Merle Grobbel, and Martin R. Stuchtey

In a world where demand for water is on the road to outstripping supply, many companies are struggling to find the water they need to run their businesses. In 2004, for instance, Pepsi Bottling and Coca-Cola closed down plants in India that local farmers and urban interests believed were competing with them for water. In 2007, a drought forced the US Tennessee Valley Authority to reduce its hydropower generation by nearly a third. Some $300 million in power generation was lost.

Businesses everywhere could face similar challenges during the next few years. A larger global population and growing economies are placing bigger demands on already-depleted water supplies. Agricultural runoff and other forms of pollution are exacerbating the scarcity of water that is clean enough for human and industrial use in some regions, and changes in climate may worsen the problem. Scarcity is raising prices and increasing the level of regulation and competition among stakeholders for access to water. To continue operating, companies in most sectors must learn how to do more with less.

Giulio Boccaletti is an associate principal in McKinsey's London office, **Merle Grobbel** is a consultant in the Zurich office, and **Martin Stuchtey** is a principal in the Munich office.

Achieving that goal is an opportunity as well as a necessity. Many of these same companies are developing products and services that can help business customers raise their water productivity. In agriculture, improved irrigation technologies and plant-management techniques are yielding "more crops per drop." New approaches now rolling out will help oil companies, mines, utilities, beverage companies, technology producers, and others use water more efficiently. Closing the gap between supply and demand by deploying water productivity improvements across regions and sectors around the world could cost, by our estimate, about $50 billion to $60 billion annually over the next two decades. Private-sector companies will account for about half of this spending, government for the rest. Many of these investments yield positive returns in just three years.

Making a business out of improving water efficiency won't be easy. Successful providers will have to migrate from selling equipment and components to selling solutions aimed at helping business customers reduce their water and energy use. The providers will therefore have to develop new skills and capabilities, particularly in marketing and sales, to identify and capture the higher-value-added solutions that business-to-business markets need. They must also engage more actively in shaping the regulations that will define this market—standing on the sidelines is no longer an option. Nearly every sector will be affected, whether a company is improving its own water productivity or selling equipment and services to help other companies do so.

Doing more with less

Many countries face a growing gap between the amount of water they can supply reliably to their economies and the amount they need. Assuming continued economic and population growth, by 2030 water supplies will satisfy only 60 percent of global demand (exhibit) and less than 50 percent in many developing regions where water supply is already under stress, including China, India, and South Africa. Closing the gap by increasing supply—through desalination, the drilling of deep wells, or transporting surface water—will be extremely difficult and expensive. More likely, governments will need to manage demand, either by raising the price of water or by capping the amount of it that users can draw.

These moves will have a direct impact on local and multinational businesses. They need water—often in large quantities—for their processes, products, and operations. Their global assets reside in countries where rules governing water usage and prices will vary, along with access to water.

Take Chile, for example—one of the world's most important mining centers and also among the driest spots on Earth. Here the authorities allocate fresh-water rights among companies strictly, closely monitor their usage of water, and pressure them to use less of it; for example,

Exhibit: **Running on empty**

By 2030, water supplies will satisfy only 60 percent of global demand on average.

Global water supply (154 basins/regions), billion cubic meters

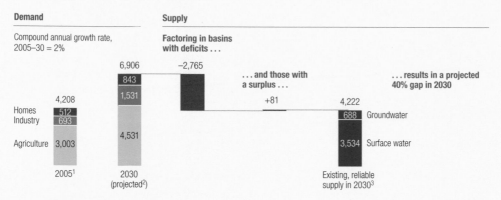

[1] Based on inputs from International Food Policy Research Institute (IFPRI).
[2] Based on frozen-technology scenario and no increase in water efficiency after 2010; figures do not sum to total, because of rounding.
[3] Supply at 90% reliability, including infrastructure investments scheduled and funded through 2010; supply in 2005 is 4,081 billion cubic meters per year, projected improvements in technology and infrastructure brings 2030 total to 4,866 billion cubic meters per year; net of environmental requirements.

Source: IFPRI; McKinsey analysis

the country's third-largest copper mine, Xstrata's Collahuasi operation, was asked to reduce its rate of water extraction to 300 liters a second by 2010, from 750 liters now. To make up the difference needed to remain in operation, the company has considered building a desalination plant or shipping in water to the mine. It is also deploying new technologies and processes, such as using less water to separate waste rock (called tailings) from ores and recycling more of the water used in the process.

Companies in several sectors are improving their water productivity. The Swedish pulp-and-paper producer SCA,[1] for instance, aims to reduce its overall water consumption by 15 percent from 2005 to 2010. SCA tracks its performance through a resource-management system that collects and aggregates data on energy, water, transport, and raw-material use, as well as waste and emission levels from both production sites and business divisions. The brewing conglomerate SABMiller launched a water footprint study to compare its total water usage, from crop to consumer, in different countries and has used the findings to target improvements throughout the value chain. By 2015, it hopes to use 25 percent less water per liter of beer produced.

Several other big corporations, such as Ford Motor Company, Nestlé, and P&G, have been reducing their water usage too. The first step is usually to study where their processes use water and how much of it. Often, these companies discover a few areas where they can make significant improvements for a small outlay. A mining company, for

[1] Svenska Cellulosa Aktiebolaget.

example, found that more than 30 percent of the expense associated with water came from potable water. By fixing leaks in a single pipeline leading to a mine, the company cut the cost of potable water by 5 percent. After examining the total costs associated with water usage, it discovered that 40 percent of them came from the energy needed to run pumps.

Few companies, however, look beyond near-term water constraints, as important as they are, to a more comprehensive assessment of the longer-term business risks associated with water scarcity. Bottling companies are among the exceptions, in part because water scarcity already influences their strategic decisions, such as where to locate operations. More and more decisions about where to put assets involve such environmental considerations.

Where the opportunities are

Many solutions that will help companies use water more efficiently in their operations—from farms to semiconductor fabs, bottling plants to nuclear ones, steel mills to oil rigs—will be new products and services under development today. Global industrial players, such as ABB, GE, and Siemens, already have large water businesses and continue to develop new products in this area for large industrial users and water utilities. IBM provides technologies to measure and track water efficiency efforts and to improve water treatment and irrigation. A few oil companies are thinking about getting into the water market by selling the pumping technology they've developed for their own operations.

Roughly speaking, the broadest range of opportunities for new products and services falls into three areas: improving the productivity of water treatment and distribution, of water-intensive industrial and power processes, or of water usage in agriculture. These segments are evolving on different time lines and involve different sets of solutions, but a broad range of companies could be successful in any of these areas.

Treatment and distribution

Municipal or private water utilities and many large businesses spend hundreds of billions of dollars a year making water fit for human consumption and industrial activity and then transporting it, through pumps and pipes, from treatment plants to points of use. The costs include expenditures on new infrastructure, such as a new treatment plants—China and India alone are building hundreds of them to treat water and wastewater—and on operating and maintaining systems. Two-thirds of this spending occurs in developed countries, but much of the growth in new systems will take place in Asia and other developing regions over the next two decades. Trillions of dollars will be spent on technology, equipment, and services.

Meeting this growth with existing technologies is a huge business in itself. In China alone, we estimate, the market for the current membrane technology used to clean wastewater will grow by more than 30 percent a year over the next two decades. Introducing new technologies and services will eventually be an even bigger opportunity, both for existing players and new entrants.

In many European and US cities, for instance, the same sewage systems collect residential and commercial wastewater, runoff rainwater, and melted snow. Singapore, by contrast, collects different gradations of discharged water separately and can redirect some of it to uses (such as watering lawns and gardens) requiring lower levels of quality. Then it goes on to treatment plants for cleaning and reuse in other applications—a far more efficient approach. In Masdar City, a planned community under construction in Abu Dhabi, urban designers hope to recycle as much as 80 percent of the water the community will use. And new desalination technologies are reducing the cost (and the extensive energy) involved in desalinating water, as well as increasing its quality. As water needs grow in the developed and developing world alike, and regulations and water prices come to reflect the need to manage demand, new solutions could provide significant value to public and private buyers.

Companies already active in this space have many opportunities to introduce new products, including devices that collect wastewater from sinks to reuse for flushing toilets, technology for collecting and reusing condensate from air-conditioning systems, more water-efficient appliances, and ultraviolet disinfection technology adapted for home use (for instance, to wash clothes with treated rainwater). Hong Kong's water department has developed systems to use seawater in toilets and may soon use it to cool commercial buildings. There are also opportunities for innovators. On the drawing board today are ideas for recycling desalinated brines, low-energy technology that separates industrial waste into irrigation-quality water and valuable chemical by-products, and ways to condense fog into usable water.

Industrial efficiency

Power and industrial companies use significant amounts of water in production processes and as a coolant—16 percent of global demand today, rising to 22 percent by 2030, with about 40 percent of this growth in China. Moving water at these volumes and using it in some processes (such as steel making or power production) requires a great deal of energy, so using less water to do more also means using less energy. One bottling company, for example, is starting to deploy a new technology, called radical water, to clean bottles.[2] The traditional process requires about five hours of cleaning; with the new one, the company can clean the same number of bottles in just 30 minutes, using significantly less water and energy.

Other technologies that can help businesses to reduce their water usage and energy costs include thickening paste tailings[3] in mines, closed-loop systems in pulp and paper plants, and flow control and automatic shut-off valves in textile production. These solutions sometimes require trade-offs, however. Dry or closed-loop cooling systems in power plants, for instance, use up to 97 percent less water but are also less efficient. (In South Africa, Eskom uses dry-cooling technology because of the looming prospect of water shortages, but in another climate the efficiency trade-offs may not make sense.) Emerging new technologies also help companies in industries such as power to use water more efficiently in energy-intensive processes. The market for these solutions will grow dramatically in just a few years as regulations and increased water prices make using large amounts of water more costly.

Finally, many manufacturers don't have the information they need to manage the water that flows through their processes—information that is critical for improving productivity. Technology providers are starting to develop products that can help these industrial companies improve the way they track their water usage and monitor their progress.

Agriculture

Farming accounts for 71 percent of global water withdrawals, a proportion that we project will decline only slightly, to 65 percent by

---

[2] Radical water, or electrochemical-activation (ECA) technology, to use its scientific name, creates unique properties in water molecules, resulting in an extremely potent yet environmentally friendly biocide. Trials and considerable R&D have proved that ECA solutions are efficacious against numerous bacteria (including MRSA), viruses, fungi (including their spores), yeasts, and many waterborne protozoa. ECA technology is particularly effective in the removal and ongoing control of biofilm, which, left unchecked, is most often responsible for the continuous contamination of the processing environment.

[3] A way to thicken tailings and any remaining process water. By 2030, this technology could save as much as 4 percent of the projected gap between water supply and demand in South Africa, or 125 million cubic meters annually. It offers savings of approximately $0.60 per cubic meter of water, with payback periods of one to two years.

2030. Water scarcity is tied both to the growing and the trading of food. India, for instance, now has just half of the water it will need in 2030, and agriculture will account for about half of the growth in water demand over the next two decades. It will account for about half of all water use in China by 2030 and for about a third in Brazil—and neither country will have enough water for all its needs in 20 years.

Finding ways to use water more efficiently in agriculture is critical. Agricultural companies are already looking for ways to design seeds and fertilizers that require less water, and better drip irrigation technologies will keep farmers from overwatering their fields. Many other sectors can provide valuable solutions under the right economic conditions. A large industrial company, for instance, could provide farming communities with pumps that it now sells to water utilities, broadening its customer base while improving efficiency in agriculture. IT solutions can help as well. They are too expensive for subsistence farmers, but water scarcity may promote consolidation and the emergence of larger farming groups that would need—and could afford—efficiency tools.

Even raising the water productivity of farms in rainy locales is a critical piece of the puzzle. Maintaining rain-fed land and improving its productivity are particularly important, since to the extent that agriculture uses water from rain, it is unnecessary to extract water for irrigation. In India, this source provides 17 percent of the total potential for agriculture to close the gap between demand and supply. The opportunities include a better fertilizer balance in fields, integrated pest management, and improved drainage systems.

Finally, financial institutions and investors can benefit from efforts to boost water productivity in treatment, efficiency, and agriculture. Banks will need to provide capital for many water productivity investments, especially when the public sector can't. The investment can be attractive for lenders, but they will have to know where and how to play. In India, for instance, some drip irrigation projects could help farmers reduce the cost of certain inputs (such as fertilizer) by up to 50 percent, depending upon the crop. Investors could capture a share of this value either as lenders or as equity holders in companies active in the drip irrigation value chain. China needs about $1.8 billion a year in capital to reduce leakage in municipal water systems. With a 22 percent rate of return, these investments could be an attractive solution for municipal utilities and their lenders alike.

Winning in water

Water is a large market, but as it grows, the rules for winning will change. Buyers of water-related goods and services, ranging across the public and private sectors, have very different needs. For many years, water has been largely a "pull" market: utilities and businesses request bids on new equipment, and the companies making it respond.

As the market grows and novel technologies become available, profitable new opportunities will emerge. Today, by meeting only the minimum standards of customers, an equipment provider has little opportunity to prove that it can give them better service, with lower costs and lower levels of risk over a life cycle. New technologies will change that.

Providers will also need to engage more actively with regulators, which over the next five years are going to design water-management policies that will determine which new technologies succeed or fail. What's more, capital costs for many projects are so high that purchases of new technologies often depend on a public buyer's ability to put together complicated deals for capital financing. Tomorrow's winners will have to tackle these issues.

Charting our water future

While meeting competing demands for water is a considerable challenge, a new report, available on mckinsey.com, provides greater clarity on the scale of that challenge and how it can be met cost effectively.

Visit mckinsey.com to read *Charting our water future*.

Developing a sales and marketing approach

Even large industrial players in the water market have found it difficult to grow in this sector. Their sales efforts, reflecting the diversity of customer segments, suffer from fragmentation across different business units. Public-sector buyers often have slow, exacting procurement processes. Corporate buyers of new water facilities often want not just components but also integrated solutions for managing water in production processes—requiring significant levels of niche-sector expertise from sellers. Highly fragmented agricultural buyers favor low-cost solutions, while desalination players are few in number and put a premium on technological innovation. Meeting these different needs requires a variety of approaches.

For this reason, large industrial suppliers typically organize their sales efforts by sector, with water-related equipment as part of the mix of solutions they provide to buyers in it. The trade-off is focus. Frequently, sales of water products take a back seat to sales efforts for higher-ticket items, such as power equipment. With no specific focus on water as a business, these suppliers feel no pressure to expand it. As a result, they are vulnerable to new entrants that specialize in the water market.

One industrial company, recognizing the opportunity to grow along with the water market, is trying to change its approach: it has created a special initiative in which sales and marketing employees across sector-based business units identify and target new opportunities. The initiative reports directly to a top executive, and team members have incentives to increase sales in water markets rather than just their respective sector-focused businesses. Over time, the company believes, a focused sales force will find new openings for higher-value services and integrated solutions.

Engage on regulation

What will shape the sector's economics, separating winners from losers, is regulation. Many water users are already actively clarifying critical positions with regulators. Water utilities, for instance, are capital-intensive businesses that make money selling water. In a world where regulators want to reduce demand for it by pricing it higher or establishing caps on its use, these utilities will need new models and a reasonable way to transition from old ones. In the United Kingdom, where water utilities have mostly been privatized, their executives are helping leaders of Ofwat, the UK Water Services Regulation Authority, to understand the nature of competition in the sector, the impact of demand management and pricing issues, and other matters that will shape the water market in coming decades. Similarly, some mining companies are working with regulators to determine the economic impact of the use of water and the options for consuming it more efficiently.

Sellers of water products and services too must participate in these debates, as some large industrial companies in the water space already do. They recognize that if regulators in a region favor water reuse as a strategy for conservation (as Singapore does), this preference will tilt the market odds in favor of companies that offer those technologies. The public-affairs units of some such companies are trying to understand how they could engage in conversations with regulators in a given region about new regulatory strategies.

We welcome your comments on this article. Please send them to quarterly_comments@ mckinsey.com.

• • •

Inescapably, water will become a strategic factor for companies in most sectors. All businesses will need to conserve, and many will make a market in conservation. Tomorrow's leaders in water productivity are getting into position today. o

An interactive exhibit, showing case studies of three countries and one region—each with its own unique set of water issues— is available on mckinseyquarterly.com.

Water as a scarce resource:

An interview with Nestlé's chairman

Peter Brabeck-Letmathe explains why water is 'by far the most valuable resource on this planet' and what we must do to conserve it.

Peter Brabeck-Letmathe, chairman of Nestlé, has repeatedly warned that water is becoming a scarce resource. Water tables are falling particularly fast in regions where agricultural output is increasing, such as in India. "The water crisis that seems possible within the next 10 to 20 years will therefore quite probably trigger significant shortfalls in cereal production and, as a result, a massive global food crisis," he says.

A member of the European Roundtable of Industrialists and of the World Economic Forum's foundation board, Brabeck-Letmathe has not been shy about using his public platforms to speak out on water issues. But what is Nestlé itself doing to conserve water? *McKinsey Quarterly* asked Peter Brabeck-Letmathe in October. His written responses to our questions follow.

The *Quarterly*: *What challenges does water scarcity pose to a company like Nestlé?*

Peter Brabeck-Letmathe: Water is, for us, a strategic issue. The main challenge is no doubt water security for the farmers who supply our factories all over the world. Farmers worldwide are the main users of water—70 percent of withdrawals, more than 90 percent of actual consumption—and they will be the most affected parties in case of a massive water shortage. In 2003, Frank Rijsberman, then the

Irrigation in a bell pepper field, Oxnard, California.

© Pete Starman/
Getty Images

head of the International Water Management Institute, had expressed his concern: "If present trends continue, the livelihoods of one-third of the world's population will be affected by water scarcity by 2025. We could be facing annual losses equivalent to the entire grain crops of India and the US combined." This is a frightening scenario. Needless to say, such a global crisis would affect all companies, not only those from the food industry.

A second challenge is the water we use in our bottling and manufacturing processes. In bottled water, quality matters much more than quantity. Quality is also key for some of our processes: water, for instance, is still one of the best solvents that we use, among other things, to gently decaffeinate coffee. Last but not least, consumers need access to safe and high-quality water to prepare many of our products.

The *Quarterly*: *What steps is Nestlé taking to address these issues?*

Peter Brabeck-Letmathe: Water has been on the Nestlé corporate agenda long before environmental policies and sustainability became an issue; the first wastewater-treatment plant for one of our factories was built back in the 1930s. Despite the fact that we are a modest water user,[1] with less than 1.8 liters per dollar of sales, we have made huge efforts to reduce water withdrawals for our factories. Withdrawals were close to 5 liters per dollar of sales some ten years ago.

[1] Both in comparison with Nestlé's competitors and, much more, with other sectors, which withdraw 120 litres or more per dollar of turnover. See *Watching Water: A Guide To Evaluating Corporate Risks in a Thirsty World*, JPMorgan, 2008; and Parry Norling, Frankie Wood-Black, and Tina M. Masciangioli, *Water and Sustainable Development: Opportunities for the Chemical Sciences*, Washington, DC: National Academies Press, 2004.

They are now below 2 liters, and we continue our efforts to further reduce them. At the same time, we make sure the water withdrawn is returned to nature in good quality.

There are other ways for us to contribute to reducing water abstraction. One is by reducing waste in the supply chain. In more concrete terms, this means doing our job and extending our efficient business processes to areas where less efficient operators are active. Let me illustrate this with an example. In a traditional milk supply chain— with open, uncooled containers from farm to consumer, on oxcarts or bikes—losses of milk are on the order of 16 to 27 percent.[2] When Nestlé collects milk directly from farmers and uses refrigerated trucks to transport it, these losses go down to less than 0.6 percent.

Based on the total amount of milk Nestlé purchases directly each year in countries such as Pakistan, India, and China (that is, in relatively difficult climatic conditions) and further on the average water require- ments for producing milk on farms, this reduction in waste means savings on the order of 815 million to 1,375 million cubic meters of water a year.[3] The total water savings on our directly purchased milk alone—thanks to our logistics, processing, and packaging—out- weigh our total annual water withdrawals (147 million cubic meters of water a year) five to eight times. And what is key: the positive impact of our efficient supply chain for milk happens to be greatest in coun- tries where the water situation is most dire.

[2] According to the UN's Food and Agriculture Organization, 16 to 25 percent of milk is lost between farms and consumer households in Tanzania (according to season) and 27 percent in Uganda.

[3] These figures cover only the milk Nestlé collects directly from farmers.

Peter Brabeck-Letmathe

Vital statistics
Born November 13, 1944, in Villach, Austria

Married, with 3 children

Education
Graduated with a degree in economics in 1968 from the University of World Trade (now Vienna University of Economics and Business)

Career highlights
Nestlé (1968–present)
• Chairman of board of directors (2005–present)
• Vice chairman of board (2001–05)
• CEO (1997–2008)
• Executive vice president (1992–97)

Fast facts
Vice chairman of the boards of L'Oréal and Credit Suisse

Awarded the Schumpeter Prize for outstanding contribution in economics (2001), and the Austrian Cross of Honour for service to the Republic of Austria

The *Quarterly*: *Would a price for water help to improve water productivity, and how would introducing such a price affect Nestlé's business?*

Peter Brabeck-Letmathe: Water—by far the most valuable resource on this planet—is treated as if did not have any value at all. We often do not even know the cost of providing it; the true number is buried under open and hidden subsidies, taxes, and the sunk costs of municipal and regional water and irrigation departments. This is particularly true for water used in agriculture. The problem is not that farmers use water; the problem is that they very frequently use it inefficiently. We see sprinklers turning at noon, unlined irrigation canals where water is seeping away faster than it actually flows, and a lack of both interest and incentives to invest in drip irrigation. Water, too often, has no price. It is seen and treated as free good, or the price for farmers is far below what others have to pay.

Full cost recovery must be implemented for all those who today get massively subsidized municipal tap water (also to fill their swimming pools) and who can actually afford to pay. This is necessary to finance the huge amount of infrastructure required to reduce leakage losses in municipal water supplies—up to 70 percent—and to provide the financial means to extend them to those who do not have access. That not only includes the close to one billion people with no access to safe water but also the far more than two billion people with access to so-called improved water sources, which in reality often means that women have to carry the daily water needs of their families some kilometers from the source to the home.[4]

What do the principles of full cost recovery mean for a company? Nestlé and the consumers of bottled water are already paying fully for the infrastructure: the bottling plant and the distribution network. Due to a lack of transparency regarding water tariffs in general, it is not always quite clear whether the tariff paid by a company for withdrawn municipal water for production and for wastewater effluent treatment always covers the full infrastructure costs. In areas where Nestlé relies on municipal water, the cost impact of an assumed increase of tariffs to, say, the levels found in Germany, would be on the order of a very small fraction of cents per dollar of our sales, based on our average of less than 1.8 liters of water withdrawn per dollar of sales. That's not very much.

Covering the full cost of water infrastructure is much more difficult for farmers. But it is also possible. In Oman, farmers draw from a

[4] See *Progress on Drinking Water and Sanitation*, UNICEF and World Health Organization, 2008.

4,500-year-old water system that is still functioning.[5] Once the water arrives at a village, from underground sources and mountain springs, channeled over many kilometers, all villagers, guests, and travelers get free access to the drinking water they need. The canal then goes to the mosque: water is also free for ceremonial washing, and some is set aside and sold to finance the mosque and the school. After that, the water becomes private property in defined shares, days, hours, or minutes of rights to use it for irrigation. The rights are inherited and, even more important, tradable. In frequent auctions, parts of the water rights can be sold and purchased or leased within the village community. If a farmer does not need water temporarily, he leases it to another farmer who has additional land available to grow a crop. If a farmer wants to invest in more efficient irrigation, he can finance this investment by selling water rights permanently. Thus, water gets a market price set by those who know best: the farmers. This is an extremely strong incentive to use water efficiently.[6] Since the market price varies over the year, this is a much smarter approach to efficiency than, for example, so-called water footprint calculations. And since farmers trade among themselves, the price places no additional financial burden on them.

The Quarterly: *At what level is leadership on this issue most critical—global or local, public or private?*

Peter Brabeck-Letmathe: Probably, local public leadership is most important. Political leaders within an area, in dialogue with the main stakeholders, have to develop and implement a clear strategy to manage water abstraction efficiently in order to overcome the risk of structural water shortages—a strategy that also includes market mechanisms. Success is possible neither piecemeal nor in isolation; it requires solutions found through multistakeholder dialogue. Success will also require full involvement and participative responsibility. At a global level, a framework is needed to make sure local measures can succeed. Among the requirements at the global level: start addressing the issue of water subsidies that risk distorting markets for the necessary flows of virtual water (embedded in farm products) between regions. Another requirement: liberalize agriculture, the sector where efficient water use is most urgent. o

[5] See an interview with Peter Brabeck-Letmathe from the World Economic Forum Annual Meeting 2008 (youtube.com/watch?v=C7smujmaMfE).
[6] See S. K. Jalota, A. Sood, J. D. Vitale, and R. Srinvasan, "Simulated crop yields response to irrigation water and economic analysis," *Agronomy Journal*, 2007, Volume 99, Issue 4, pp. 1073–84.

By Invitation: Insights and opinion from outside contributors

Next-generation water policy for businesses and government

The solution to water scarcity, in part, will come from new technologies for better managing water as a resource. But to make these technologies more effective, business and policy leaders will need to work more closely to implement them.

John Briscoe

John Briscoe is the Gordon McKay Professor of the Practice of Environmental Engineering at Harvard University and is on the faculty of the schools of engineering and applied sciences, government, and public health.

Water insecurity looms as one of the great challenges of the 21st century, and it is one that policy makers and business leaders must face together. Policy makers recognize that certain technologies being developed by leading companies are critical tools for effectively managing scarce water supplies. But business leaders must do more to help shape the understanding of how good policies make it possible for technologies to be productive—and how ineffective ones do the reverse.

Public-sector leaders and nongovernmental organizations (NGOs) have long dominated the debate on water policy, but within the last five years, a growing number of progressive private-sector companies have also started to lend their perspectives on how best to effectively manage water. These companies have begun by paying much more attention to the water environment in which they function. As they develop a new generation of water-related technologies, they also increasingly influence a new generation of public policies that stimulate the development and use of these technologies. Here is how a number of them are engaging along both of these dimensions.

One group of companies, including beverage, mining, and energy businesses, has found that growing water scarcity constitutes a threat

Desalination plant in
Carboneras, Spain.

© Georg Fischer/
Bilderberg/Aurora

to their social license to operate. In response, some have made large donations to activist groups in the hopes of buying peace. Others have asked for water standards that they can then meet in their plants. The most far-sighted of these companies, however—with Nestlé as a leading example—recognize that while companies have to manage water efficiently behind their factory gate, society (along with companies and their suppliers) needs an equitable, efficiency-stimulating, and predictable legal and regulatory environment that governs all water uses. These companies also believe that private businesses have useful and legitimate inputs to make into the policy-formulation process, and that good business practices can guide effective implementation.

A second group of companies is developing technologies that can enable society to get more product—more food, energy, income, employment—per drop of water. There are three broad segments. The first comprises companies that develop productivity-enhancing seeds and agricultural technologies. Because agriculture accounts for more than 80 percent of water consumption in the developing world and because the productivity gains of the last round of agricultural technologies (the "green revolution") have fallen to less than 1 percent a year (from about 3 percent a year in the 1960s), these innovations are vital for better water management. The importance of genetically modified organism (GMO) crops—a core agricultural technology— is illustrated by the contrasting performance of corn in Europe, where GMOs are not allowed, and in Iowa, where 90 percent of corn is grown from using GMOs. In the last ten years, corn yields in Europe have stagnated, while in the United States productivity has grown at over 2 percent a year. Existing GMOs already use substantially lower amounts of fertilizers, pesticides, and water. And some new-generation crops will be better able to thrive despite water stress.

A second segment of companies is developing new technologies for treating water and wastewater. The process of desalination illustrates the importance in this area. The laws of thermodynamics state that it is theoretically possible to desalinate seawater by using only 25 percent of the energy currently required to do so through exist-ing technologies. If new developments in, for example, nanotechnology and membranes allow even half of this potential to be realized, the cost of desalination will fall to a level where most cities and indus-tries in coastal areas through-out the world can turn to it as the new source of choice. The third segment comprises companies that provide users with just-in-time and just-what's-needed information—such as on the probability of rainfall, on soil moisture, on water, and on fertilizer requirements. This is essen-tial for energy consumption, domestic use of water, and, most impor-tant, for agriculture. Precision agriculture can produce much more crop per drop than traditional methods can, and industries and cities can use much less water too.

Related articles on mckinseyquarterly.com

Meeting the challenges of China's growing cities

What countries can do about cutting carbon emissions

Going from global trends to corporate strategy

Executives at these leading companies know that progress in water management depends on linked advancement in technologies and policies. They have seen instances in some countries where policy shortcomings mean that many existing technologies that make more efficient use of water are not being fully employed. This has prompted a growing number of companies to engage with policy makers to ensure that key policies—such as tradeable water rights, support for intellectual-property rights, and efficiency-enhancing regulation—are implemented. In conversations with policy makers, corporate leaders highlight examples like the Murray-Darling Basin, in Australia, where an enabling policy environment means that a 70 percent reduction in water availability has had virtually no impact on agricultural production. In situations like this, policy makers know that what is needed is a "next generation" of technologies that will enable society to do more with less. And they know that the key to achieving this is a legal and business policy environment that stimulates the development of the next generation of water efficiency technologies.

We welcome your comments on this article. Please send them to quarterly_comments@ mckinsey.com.

Although the glass may certainly look half empty, it is also half full, not least because progressive business leaders understand that water scarcity is an issue that will affect their industries, suppliers, and the communities in which they work—and they've stepped into the policy area to help shape solutions. And as they have, policy leaders have begun to better understand the private-sector's contributions and to draft more effective enabling regulations. But more business and policy leaders need to follow the lead of their progressive colleagues. That is how we will secure further development of new technologies and the formulation and implementation of a new generation of water-management policies. o

Managing water strategically:

An interview with the CEO of Rio Tinto

Tom Albanese explains how Rio Tinto is adapting its operations to prepare for a future when climate change may make the world's dry parts drier and the wet parts wetter.

Bill Javetski

Water management has become a strategic issue for Rio Tinto, one of the world's largest mining groups, whose operations tend to be located in areas that are either arid or plagued by torrential rains. In this interview, adapted from a video conversation available on mckinseyquarterly.com, CEO Tom Albanese discusses the economics of water, the role of climate change, and how Rio Tinto is seeking to make water management a source of advantage.

The Quarterly: *Global population growth and economic growth are putting a strain on water resources around the world. What are the challenges that this poses to Rio Tinto?*

Tom Albanese: For Rio Tinto, water has long been a strategic issue. At our operations, once the ore has been mined, process facilities extract or refine the products—which include copper, iron ore, coal, and many others—prior to sale. Through this process, the businesses that we're in tend to consume a lot of water. So we have to develop long-term, sustainable approaches that can provide the water we need in a way that meets the wide range of stakeholder expectations in many locations, which are predominantly quite arid.

Bill Javetski is a member of *McKinsey Quarterly*'s board of editors.

The Quarterly: *What are the components of your strategy for dealing with a scarcity of water resources?*

Tom Albanese: What we find—and we have the same issue with carbon emissions—is that there are some limitations on how much you can actually do in an existing facility, because certain processes simply use a lot of water. Looking forward, the most important part of our strategy will probably be to ensure that future facilities that we build or future mines that we develop are actually designed, from the very beginning, using the principles of water conservation. To some extent, we have to begin thinking about pricing for that water, even if only on an internal basis.

The *Quarterly*: *How do you think about the economics of water?*

Tom Albanese: I do think, as we look forward, we'll recognize that water generally will have a regional mechanism for management. But it has to have global linkages to a broader strategy. We will work on the basis that, ultimately, there'll be a need for some pricing of water—some way to make the appropriate capital trade-offs for water efficiencies.

In many locations, this happens by itself. For example, we're in a joint venture at Minera Escondida, in northern Chile, which is a very dry location. So we have one of the larger desalination facilities in South America, which we just constructed over the past two years. It is a large energy consumer. So, again, water links back with energy. As you're accessing additional water, you're beginning to access the scarce energy that's available. We're taking seawater that we cannot use directly in our processes, converting it to fresh water, and then using that within the facility. That, by itself, creates a pricing for the water—it's the price of the energy, the price of the desalination, and

Tom Albanese

Vital statistics
Born September 9, 1957, in Akron, Ohio

Married, with 2 children

Education
Graduated with a BS in mineral economics and an MS in mining engineering from the University of Alaska Fairbanks

Career highlights
Rio Tinto (1993–present)
• CEO (2007–present)
• CEO, copper group; head of exploration (2004–07)
• CEO, industrial minerals group (2000–04)

Fast facts
Has served on the boards of Ivanhoe Mines (2006–07), Palabora Mining Company (2004–06), and the International Copper Association (2004–06)

Enjoys canal boating, reading, and walking

Main pit at the Rio Tinto iron ore mine at Tom Price, about 800 miles north of Perth, Australia.

© Christian Sprogoe

the price of the pumping. That will lead to the mine having a greater incentive to conserve water in the future. This is a good example of how efficient market mechanisms, once they're in place, will contribute to water conservation.

The *Quarterly*: *What are the overlaps between the water scarcity issue and the broader issue of climate change and carbon?*

Tom Albanese: One of the overlaps between carbon and water would be the general assumption, which we embrace, that with climate change, dry parts of the world will get drier and wet parts will get wetter. This means, for us, that water management and water conservation in the dry locations will be increasingly important. So we will need, increasingly, to build the costs of water into any future investment decisions, which is what we've done at the corporate level. We've said, "If we are going to build a new mine, we have to have—within that mine operation, within that process—a very specific water strategy." But in other locations in the world, you have to manage the water from large rainfalls or storms. Those storm events will get bigger and more violent, and they will put more water into our mine systems and our mine property in very short, intense periods of time. So we will have to adapt our operations for drier areas getting drier and wetter areas getting wetter.

To watch a video of a panel discussion among Rio Tinto's Tom Albanese, Chesapeake Energy's Aubrey McClendon, and Scana's Bill Timmerman—in which the three CEOs offer their perspectives on the scientific, resource, and policy issues challenging energy sustainability today—visit mckinseyquarterly.com.

The *Quarterly:* *How much of an investment does this represent for a company of Rio Tinto's size?*

Tom Albanese: Water is a strategic constraint, and we will see it having an effect on the capital costs of projects. I can think of at least five projects in the planning stages right now where, if you were to rank risks, water—either not having enough or having too much—would be in the top five categories that need to be taken into consideration in terms of the design of the facility. For example, if we have ore stockpiles or leaching pads in wet areas, we will have to spend more money on water-containment systems. And it's not just a few millions of dollars. It could be hundreds of millions of dollars more for water management, in anticipation of what formerly would have been called a hundred-year rain event actually happening every four or five years.

The *Quarterly:* *Is your investment in resources to handle water scarcity a cost of doing business? Or is there a return on investment that you see from this?*

Tom Albanese: I think it's an enabler to doing business. I think that having the ability to manage responsibly in areas of water scarcity is an enabler to being in those operations in the first place. Having the ability to manage excessive water, particularly if it's coming in extreme storm events, is also an enabler.

We've definitely created a unique skill set. It's interesting because I've had some engineering companies come to me and say, "You know, you've been poaching our people. They heard about your water-management programs in Australia, and they're really excited to be working with them." So I do think that for those water-management specialists, we can create an attractive employment proposition, which can allow us to build greater competencies. Going forward, we continue to have more work to do within our own operations all over the world. ○

Jean-François Martin

Strategy

Sustainability and the CEO

In the wake of the economic crisis, companies are emerging battered and consumers disillusioned; responsibility for the fallout has led to the door of the C-suite. As businesses try to right themselves and their public image, they face a customer base with waning trust and ever-rising expectations.

The articles in this package discuss the changing role of business in society and the ways senior executives are addressing the important social issues of the day. As more companies must rethink their business models in the face of threatened natural resources and increasing levels of concern about climate change, sustainability is quickly becoming a crucial business imperative. Companies that invest in it and in corporate social responsibility programs can improve both their profitability and their reputations.

Building a sustainable Ford Motor Company:

An interview with Bill Ford

The carmaker's executive chairman talks about
sustainability and technological change.

Sheila Bonini and Hans-Werner Kaas

William Clay Ford, Jr., has long been a strong advocate, inside Ford
Motor Company, of winning through sustainability. Profits will rise,
argues the automaker's executive chairman and the great-grandson of
Henry Ford, as it delivers vehicles that are better for the environment,
made in plants that are increasingly energy efficient and, consequently,
less costly to operate. For years, few in the company seemed to fully
embrace this vision. But in the wake of rising oil prices and a
global economic crisis, management has rallied behind it. In October
2009, Ford discussed his views in an interview, excerpted here,
with McKinsey's Sheila Bonini and Hans-Werner Kaas.

The *Quarterly*: *You've long advocated sustainability. How did you
come to these views?*

Sheila Bonini is a
consultant in McKinsey's
Silicon Valley office, and
Hans-Werner Kaas is
a director in the Detroit
office.

Bill Ford: My leanings go back to college. When I joined Ford, in the
late 1970s, I felt strongly we could not forever be a huge user of natural
resources without consequences. But I was alone. Through the '80s,
I tried to find kindred spirits within Ford. There were a few, but it was
an uphill battle. Top management thought I was probably a Bolshevik.
I never wanted Ford to be a place, like the tobacco industry, where

employees were not proud of coming to work. Our business, like others, depends on getting the best and brightest, and we wouldn't get them if this place was not socially acceptable to work at.

When I joined the board, in 1988, I was told I couldn't have any environmental leanings. I completely disregarded that. Someone had to build a bridge between the environmental community and the business community. I think I was the first executive to ever speak at a Greenpeace business conference, in 2001. That didn't play well here at Ford, but it was an important signal to send internally.

The *Quarterly*: *What generated the resistance?*

Bill Ford: With gas cheaper than bottled water, there wasn't a great pull in the marketplace for fuel-efficient vehicles. Also, traditionally, such vehicles were seen as cheap and not fun to drive. Now fuel prices have risen, and the technology has developed to the point where we can give customers great fuel economy and a great driving experience. We can say we want to be the fuel economy leader in every segment we participate in—and that does not scare people internally.

The *Quarterly*: *How did you change internal perceptions?*

Bill Ford: Among other things, I pointed to what happened in Europe. Customers there made the switch to smaller cars and more efficient

Bill Ford

Vital statistics
Born May 3, 1957, in Detroit, Michigan

Married, with 4 children

Education
Graduated with a BA in history in 1979 from Princeton University

Earned MBA in 1984 from MIT

Career highlights
Ford Motor Company (1979–present)
• Appointed executive chairman (2006)
• Appointed CEO (2001)
• Elected chairman of board of directors (1999)
• Elected chairman of finance committee (1995)
• Joined company as a product-planning analyst (1979)

Fast facts
Is an avid fly fisherman and car enthusiast, plays hockey and tennis, and is a black belt in tae kwon do

The full version of this interview is available on mckinseyquarterly.com.

fuel—in that case, diesel. And small cars in Europe were well appointed and fun to drive. They had a very good performance capability.

But one thing that is lacking in this country that could make the European model work is a convening entity. In Europe, all the players got around the table—the NGOs,[1] governments, and automakers. There wasn't unanimity, but there was a lot of dialogue, and a target was agreed upon. Here, we have government, NGOs, and manufacturers all lobbing bombs at each other. Whether it's the electric highway, biofuels, or diesel, the auto industry can't unilaterally

[1] Nongovernmental organizations.

Making sustainability real

Sheila Bonini and
Stephan Görner

Ford Motor Company is one of many—in sectors from consumer goods to concrete manufacturing to Internet services—that have launched environmental-sustainability initiatives. But few companies pursue this goal comprehensively across the organization. In our experience, sustainability commitments achieve a real impact—significant reductions in carbon emissions, say, or dramatic improvements in water or energy efficiency or in waste management—by ensuring executive accountability for these efforts, coordinating them across the enterprise, and communicating the value of what's achieved both to top managers and investors.

Managing sustainability begins and ends with the accountability of senior executives. In a recent study, less than 13 percent of Russell 1000 companies reported having an executive-level committee responsible for sustainability efforts, and less than 6 percent had a C-level executive on the hook for making progress in this area.[1] Lacking this kind of accountability, companies struggle to integrate sustainability into their core planning effectively and to make the right decisions about allocating resources to get the job done. Moreover, when senior executives don't visibly wave the flag for sustainability, the organization—probably rightly—infers that this is not a strategic priority.

Without senior leadership, it is also difficult for companies to pursue coordinated, organization-wide sustainability initiatives. Improvements

may bubble up from the middle—a plant manager committed to reducing energy use or a country manager who has to address water scarcity issues—but they are typically fragmented responses. In these companies, it is challenging for an executive even to know the carbon or water footprint, much less identify how to make improvements.

Worse, uncoordinated efforts can act at cross-purposes. One large packaged-goods company, for example, sought opportunities to reduce the impact of its packaging, but much of the cost-savings and environmental potential remained on the table because sourcing managers took into account only the procurement costs of smaller packaging. Other factors that could enhance the company's sustainability efforts, such as packaging designs that would take up less space in inventory or weigh less (and thus cost less to transport), were left unaddressed. The lack of broad metrics and targets meant that senior-level management did not have enough visibility to make strategic sustainability decisions from procurement through the customer experience.

Finally, senior executives lack accountability for sustainability in part because most companies don't track the financial impact of these activities. Companies also don't communicate their impact to senior managers or to the market. In general, investors believe that sustainability can add to a company's bottom line, but they don't always understand the

Sheila Bonini is a consultant in McKinsey's Silicon Valley office, and **Stephan Görner** is a principal in the Sydney office.

solve these issues. We need collaboration, which is not something, in this country, that has traditionally happened.

The Quarterly: *What else did you do?*

Bill Ford: At the River Rouge plant, we took the world's largest brownfield site and made it into the world's greenest assembly plant. At Rouge, we're turning paint fumes into energy. We have grass roofs on some of our plants. We have permeable parking lots, so that storm waters sink into the ground. We're applying lots of technologies—some

full financial value of these efforts, because executives don't track and communicate it to them. A recent McKinsey survey of investors and CFOs found general agreement among both groups that sustainability activities could potentially generate shareholder value, but in practice both say that they don't take this possibility into consideration very much when they evaluate business investments.[2] This problem sets up a vicious cycle: markets have less opportunity to value sustainability efforts because there are fewer of them, which in turn prompts investors and CFOs to view them as projects that generate less value than other business initiatives do.

Accountability, coordination, and communication are mutually reinforcing. Waste Management, FedEx, and Dow Chemical, among other companies, have shown how to harness these three critical factors. At Waste Management, for example, CEO Dave Steiner oversaw organization-wide strategic planning to find ways of profiting from sustainability activities. That review led Waste Management to increase the focus on its recycling business, on turning waste to energy, and on increasing the fuel efficiency of its trucks. The company tracks and manages progress in all these areas and communicates its achievements within the company and, externally, to investors.

Senior executives at FedEx led efforts to improve the fuel efficiency of its fleet of planes and vehicles and to use more alternative

energy. They also propelled the organization to think innovatively about sustainability and the customer value proposition. Now, rather than shipping documents across the country, for example, client companies can have them sent electronically to a FedEx Office store near the destination, printed there, and then delivered locally. This approach leads to notably lower emissions—and cost savings as well.

At Dow Chemical, executives are overseeing development of a second set of ten-year goals for company-wide sustainability (to 2015, building on a first set of goals originally developed in 1994). Both plans not only address key sustainability challenges but are also driving the creation of significant financial value. Dow has invested $1 billion, for instance, from 1994 to 2005 to reduce its energy consumption and improve its water and energy productivity, reaping $4.3 billion in cost savings. Savings have continued to accrue from these efforts, amounting to over $8.6 billion by the end of 2008.

[1] *The Road Not Taken: The State of US Corporate Environmental Policy and Management*, Sustainable Enterprise Institute, 2007.

[2] "Valuing corporate social responsibility: McKinsey Global Survey Results," mckinseyquarterly.com, February 2009.

high tech, some low tech. One low-tech thing we've done is to use plants to suck up dirty water. Working with Michigan State University, we tested the hypothesis that if you dump heavy metals into the right kind of field, plants will suck it up, and what comes out the other end is drinking-quality water. At Rouge, that has worked very well, yet it's very cost effective.

A lot of these things were big cost savers, as well as right for the environment. One thing I realized all along was that if sustainability was just an expensive showcase, it would never work. It had to make sense from a business standpoint, and you had to demonstrate that. Not everything does, frankly. But there's now general agreement, within the company, that we need to keep pushing (for more, see sidebar, "Making sustainability real").

> 'One thing I realized all along was that if sustainability was just an expensive showcase, it would never work'

We won't be the laggard. Whichever avenue proves to be predominant—electric or biofuels or hydrogen or diesel—we will be there with the hardware. During the difficult years from 2006 to 2008, I insisted we keep our R&D spending in all these areas. Many of our competitors cut back. Now we are emerging, hopefully, in a better market, with a leadership position in many key technologies.

The *Quarterly*: *Was there a moment when you knew the mind-set was shifting?*

Bill Ford: Probably the seminal event was when Derrick Kuzak, head of global product development, took all the disparate product-development centers around the world and slammed them together. That also allowed him to drive this sustainability philosophy through the whole product-development system, in a way that would have been impossible before. Inside Ford, however, we don't use the term sustainability very much, because it lacks clarity. We talk about being the fuel economy leader, about which technology is going to drive that, and about cleaning our plants up and applying technology to our facilities to drive carbon dioxide emissions out.

The *Quarterly*: *But you issue a sustainability report.*

Bill Ford: We were one of the first industrial companies to do so. When I first introduced that report, around 2000, I was blasted by the business press. They asked, "Why would you criticize your own performance?" I personally came under a lot of criticism. People thought I was an idiot. Now it's become much more widely accepted.

For us, sustainability is not just about the environment—if you don't have a sustainable business model, none of the rest matters. Sustainability is also about having the right employees.

The Quarterly: *With so many paths—improved internal-combustion engines, electric cars, biofuels, hydrogen—how do you manage uncertainty?*

Bill Ford: Ford celebrated its 100th anniversary in 2003. For 100 years, pretty much all we had was the internal-combustion engine. Now we stand at the threshold of some real technological revolutions. In the medium term, we will certainly have a mix.

For all these new systems, you get national infrastructure issues. If it's going to be electricity, how do we get a true "smart" grid, for example? We have some interesting pilot programs, with various utilities, that have been very encouraging, but to replicate that on a national scale is a tall order. If it's going to be hydrogen, you're going to have to tear up every corner gas station, and you will have storage issues on site and on vehicles. Shipping hydrogen to stations is another challenge. As for biofuels, they tend not to ship through pipelines. I think you'll have very localized production of ethanol—or other biofuels—that will ship locally.

Related articles on mckinseyquarterly.com
Tackling sociopolitical issues in hard times
Valuing social responsibility
CEOs on strategy and social issues

All of that will require a big tear-up to our infrastructure, and I'm not sure this country can take more than one big tear-up. So at some point, as a nation, we will have to place our bets.

The Quarterly: *Do you have a gut feeling how this might break?*

Bill Ford: Today, I'd say electric. But 18 months ago, I would have said biofuels, and 18 months before that I would have said hydrogen. Things are changing quickly. There is always a technology darling of the moment. We need to make sure that we're not only abreast of all these technologies but trying to lead in all of them—and also staying abreast of developing technologies. We can't be the last ones figuring things out.

The *Quarterly*: *How is this influencing the way Ford innovates?*

Bill Ford: We have some really bright award-winning scientists. For many years, they felt frustrated by a disconnect between what they did and what came out in the marketplace. Now they are seeing flow-through from what they do into our products, and they love that. This is not just on sustainability; it's on safety, traffic and real-time parking information, and other things. Also, we're collaborating a lot more with universities and our suppliers because we don't have a monopoly on good ideas.

The *Quarterly*: *Looking ahead five years, what else do you want for Ford?*

We welcome your comments on this article. Please send them to quarterly_comments@ mckinsey.com.

Bill Ford: I hope we will be recognized by customers as a leader in the application of technology that makes their lives better. I also hope we will be seen nationally as a key player in the dialogue about where the United States is headed as a nation. We need to work hard, to stay humble, and to remember that we're never where we want to be.○

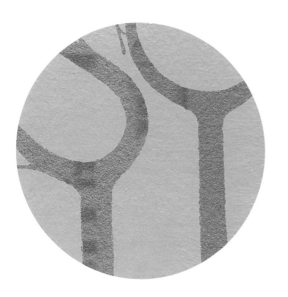

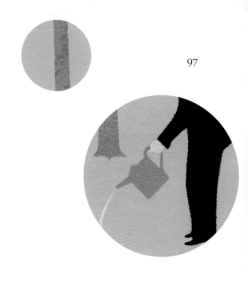

Leading through values: An interview with Paul Polman of Unilever

The company's CEO shares his thoughts on social responsibility, mentorship, and leading in a crisis.

Adam Bird

Paul Polman took on the role of CEO at Unilever in January 2009, during the eye of the financial storm. After holding high positions at both P&G and Nestlé, Polman's move to Unilever has given him the rare vantage point of one who has served as an executive at three of the world's largest fast-moving consumer goods companies. In this excerpt from an interview series *McKinsey conversations with global leaders*, Polman reflects on the importance of corporate social responsibility and values-based management, on the role of mentorship, and on how he defines leadership. Adam Bird, a director in McKinsey's Munich office, conducted this interview in London in September 2009.

The *Quarterly*: *You've had significant experience as a top executive at P&G, Nestlé, and now Unilever. What have you picked up from each one of these different places?*

Adam Bird is a director in McKinsey's Munich office.

Paul Polman: I think the main thing is that these are all great companies, driven by strong values. And these are companies that are becoming increasingly more appreciated for the role they play

This interview is excerpted from a broader discussion that is part of the series *McKinsey conversations with global leaders*. To watch a video or download a PDF of the full interview, visit mckinseyquarterly.com.

in shaping the economy, even more so than before. So, I think these values permeate these companies: doing the right thing for the long term, operating with a high level of integrity and trust, investing in their people, wanting the communities where they operate to be as successful as the companies themselves. Purpose and values are very important. One thing I've learned over the course of my career is that if your values—your personal values— are aligned with the company's values, you're probably going to be more successful in the long term than if they are not. Because if they aren't, it requires you to be an actor when you go to work or to have a split personality.

The *Quarterly*: *A key element of a values-driven corporation is contributing both to society and to a broad range of stakeholders. As someone who is very engaged in a number of social causes, how do you see that role evolving?*

Paul Polman: Well, I think it is absolutely crucial, and even more important in today's environment. I think we've learned the lessons from the last year and a half—what greed and mismanagement, to some extent, can lead to. And here, in some sectors, how it can affect society at large and, often, people who cannot do anything about it themselves.

It was Viktor Frankl who was an unfortunate victim of Nazi Germany and survived. He wrote a book, *Man's Search for Meaning*, in which he said that what we forgot to do when we erected the Statue of Liberty on the East Coast was to erect a Statue of Responsibility on the West Coast.

And it is very clear that this world faces tremendous challenges. The challenges of poverty, of water, of global warming, of climate change. And businesses like ours have a role to play in that—and frankly, to me, a very appealing one. Every day, in our business, we have about two billion consumers who use our brands, and so there is a tremendous opportunity to reach many consumers. And if we do the right thing, leveraging that tremendous skill, we can actually make major progress in society.

At Unilever, we've translated that very simply into our brands. Because at the end of the day, our brands need to grow, but we think it's very important that our brands have what we call "the social missions." Ben and Jerry's is a good example of that; they are a key player in addressing climate change and the use of nuclear weapons. But we have other brands: Lipton with the Rainforest Alignment on sustainable tea, and Dove with women's health awareness—the list goes on. So, brands have a very important role to play. And obviously, the organization itself, the brand Unilever—or, for other companies, their brand—is becoming increasingly important as well.

And to be honest, in today's environment we see the consumer asking for this. Again, the consumer's trust in business, unfortunately, is lower than we would like it to be. And the standards that the consumer sets—the expectations, her own proactiveness and influencing with her purchase decisions, and her own beliefs—are only going to increase as we move forward, I believe (see sidebar, "Toward meeting consumer expectations"). So, companies with a strong social mission will be companies that are more successful in the long term.

The *Quarterly*: *Do you see that as a long-term process? Gaining trust back is often a painful, extended effort.*

Paul Polman: Well, I tend to believe that we start from a strong base in Unilever, but it's true that you cannot talk yourself out of things you've behaved yourself into. Trust is easily destroyed and takes a long time to rebuild. We've clearly focused on a few areas where we believe we can make a difference.

We focus on sustainable sourcing. We've made a commitment to switch to sustainable palm oil, and we're sourcing all of our vegetables sustainably. That's a major need, to ensure that we have continuity of sourcing. But palm oil—sustainable palm oil—deforestation is 15 to 20 percent of the global warming. So, there you have a broader influence than just our products. We focus on nutrition and hygiene, for obvious reasons, and then we focus on water. And those are the areas that affect our business, but also the areas where we think we can make a positive contribution.

The *Quarterly*: *Who have been great mentors to you as you've evolved?*

Paul Polman: Well, I've always been fortunate to be able to bounce off ideas with people whom I have respected. And, obviously, you have your family members. My first boss, who unfortunately has passed on, was a tremendous mentor. I've had people whom I have looked up to, and, of course, history is full of mentors.

Toward meeting consumer expectations

Sheila Bonini

Paul Polman isn't the only executive who believes that even as trust in business has fallen to new lows, consumers' expectations for business's role in society have risen. A majority of C-level executives McKinsey surveyed recently said that the importance of tackling challenges whose impact extends beyond the walls of the corporation had increased as a result of the global economic turmoil. In another recent survey, executives also highlighted two issues—compensation and governance—that have figured less prominently in past years (presumably because they were seen as private-business matters) but that have grown in the public eye in the wake of both the financial crisis and taxpayer-funded bailouts in some countries and sectors.[1]

Despite the perception that the public cares more now about business's relationship with society, only 6 percent of C-level survey respondents said they thought senior executives were playing a leadership role in addressing social issues—the same share as said so in a 2007 survey. And more than two-thirds said the financial crisis and subsequent global recession hadn't changed their own behavior in this area.

This disconnection between public expectations and the actions of business leaders could lead to a consumer or regulator backlash. Our surveys and experience also suggest that companies that don't act on social and environmental issues could be forgoing other hard business benefits—such as access to new markets or workforce efficiency—not to mention the favor of investors, who, our research indicates, do place a value on corporate social responsibility.[2] What's more, managing these issues successfully requires a coordinated organizational approach that many companies lack, underlining the importance of senior leaders' involvement. When senior leaders themselves become involved with initiatives that address these issues, they not only send a strong signal to external stakeholders and the public, their involvement also helps stress the issue's importance to executives inside the organization, which in turn motivates them to work across functional barriers to address these issues.

Sheila Bonini is a consultant in McKinsey's Silicon Valley office.

I think if you look at the Gandhis and the Mandelas and the Mother Teresas, I think they exhibit a form of leadership that is very appealing to me, which is to put the interest of others ahead of oneself. It's obvious leadership. Jim Collins talked about level-five leadership in his book *Good to Great*.[1] And I think that that these people are actually able to make it come alive.

Related articles on mckinseyquarterly.com

McKinsey conversations with global leaders: John Chambers of Cisco

Rebuilding corporate reputations

Nurturing entrepreneurship in India's villages

I'm very inspired by, for example, the Dalai Lama, who said once, "If you seek enlightenment for yourself just to enhance yourself, you missed the purpose. If you seek enlightenment for yourself by helping others, you are with purpose." And I think that's the style of leadership that we increasingly need in today's world.

[1] Jim Collins, *Good to Great*, New York: HarperCollins, 2001.

So how can executives get started? Businesses can't simply address public expectations with a smattering of philanthropic or corporate social responsibility programs. And a company won't get credit for good deeds if it is struggling with ethics and governance issues, with questions about how it treats its customers or employees, or with concerns about its behavior on social and environmental issues where the public sees it as 'part of the problem.' One example of this dynamic at work can be seen in the tele-communications sector, where initiatives aimed at tackling problems such as the digital divide—through the creation of public–private partnerships that provide rural communities with telecom access, for example—can be obscured by consumer questions about surcharges and fees.

Depending on a company's situation, the first order of business might be to increase trans-parency significantly or to address social and environmental issues that are the most relevant to its business. Best Buy, for example, in a proactive effort to address the challenge of how to safely dispose of electronics components,

launched an e-waste recycling program to provide customers with the opportunity to bring their old electronics to Best Buy stores to be recycled. The program provides convenience for customers and positions the company as an environmental leader among consumers and regulators—all the while encouraging shoppers to visit its stores.

In addition, philanthropic or corporate social responsibility programs that reinforce a company's other efforts to enhance its relationship with society can earn a company significant reputational capital. In the high-tech sector, for example, Cisco Systems, IBM, and Microsoft all invest in education and in providing tech-nology to developing markets. These initiatives help cultivate a positive reputation today and have the potential to help build new markets and enlarge the talent pool in the future.

[1] "Tackling sociopolitical issues in hard times: McKinsey Global Survey results," mckinseyquarterly.com, September 2009.
[2] "Valuing corporate social responsibility: McKinsey Global Survey Results," mckinseyquarterly.com, February 2009.

The _Quarterly_: _And that is how you would define leadership? That's your personal definition that has emerged for you?_

Paul Polman: Well, I don't have a personal leadership definition, because, as I said, there are different styles of leadership. But actually, everybody is a leader, as far as I'm concerned. And my definition of leadership is very simple: if you positively influence someone, you are a leader. I was in Kenya recently, and there was a girl—12 years old—starting a program in her school for the HIV-infected students, which there were quite a lot of. She was a leader.

At the same time, the teacher who took on these responsibilities—often there are few in those places, and they earn maybe $100 a month—she is a leader. And so, there are many, many leaders that we have, that make our society work. And I think the main thing is that people can be themselves. And I do it by a strong, as I said, inner com-pass and guidance. That is more important than anything else. ○

Risk: Seeing around the corners

Risk-assessment processes typically expose only the
most direct threats facing a company and neglect
indirect ones that can have an equal or greater impact.

Eric Lamarre and Martin Pergler

The financial crisis provided a valuable reminder that risks gone
bad in one part of the economy can set off chain reactions in areas that
may seem completely unrelated. Organizations that thought they
had a handle on risk management are no longer certain of their ability
to anticipate the effects, both positive and negative, of events that
occur throughout the business cycle.

There's no easy formula for anticipating the path of risk as it cascades
through a company or an economy. But we've found that executives who systematically examine the way risks propagate across the
whole value chain—including competitors, suppliers, distribution
channels, and customers—can foresee and prepare for indirect threats
more successfully.

Eric Lamarre is a
director in McKinsey's
Montréal office, where
Martin Pergler is a
consultant.

The benefits of that approach can be substantial, and not just for companies whose businesses are deeply intertwined with the global

Neil Webb

financial markets. When a lightning strike set off a fire at a microchip plant in New Mexico in 2000, for example, it damaged millions of chips slated for use in mobile phones from a number of manufacturers. Companies that were prepared quickly shifted their sourcing to different US and Japanese suppliers. Others couldn't and lost hundreds of millions of dollars in sales.

A risk-management framework

What differentiates winners from losers in such situations is the ability to look—ahead of time—beyond immediate, obvious risks, and to evaluate aftereffects that could destabilize whole value chains. Most companies have some sort of process to identify and rank threats, often as part of an enterprise risk-management program. But few companies thoroughly analyze the dangers arising from all of their direct and indirect business relationships with critical stakeholders (Exhibit 1). Organizations that keep the full range of stakeholders in mind are likely to be better prepared.

Competitors

Often, the most important area to investigate is the way events might change a company's cost position versus its competitors or substitute products. Different business models, particularly around currency exposures, supply bases, or cost structures, naturally create the potential for a competitive risk exposure, favorable or unfavorable. The point isn't that a company should imitate its competitors but rather that it should think about the risks it implicitly assumes when its strategy departs from theirs. Consider, for example, the impact of fuel price hedging on fares in the highly competitive airline industry. If the airlines covering a certain route don't hedge, changes in fuel costs tend to percolate quickly through to customers—either directly, as higher fares, or indirectly, as fuel surcharges. By contrast, if the airlines covering that route are fully hedged, that would offset changes in fuel prices, so fares probably wouldn't move. But if some airlines hedge and others don't, fuel price increases force the nonhedgers to take a significant hit in margins or market share while the hedgers make windfall profits.

Supply chains

Classic cascading effects linked to supply chains include disruptions in the availability of parts or raw materials, changes in the cost structures of suppliers, and shifts in logistics costs. When the price of oil reached $150 a barrel in 2008, for example, many offshore suppliers became substantially less cost competitive in the US market. Consider the case of steel. Since Chinese imports were the marginal price setters in the United States, prices for steel rose 20 percent there as the cost of shipping it from China went up by nearly $100 a ton.

The fact that logistics costs depend significantly on oil prices is hardly surprising, but most steel companies were focused only on direct threats, in this case the price of steel itself. Few of them—even companies where fluctuating costs may well have been one of the biggest risk factors—considered their indirect exposure to oil prices through the supply chain.

Distribution channels

Indirect risks can also lurk in distribution channels, where cascading effects interfere with deliveries to customers, change distribution costs, or even radically redefine business models, as happened when broadband Internet access roiled the music-recording industry. Likewise, consider the effects of the bankruptcy and liquidation of the US consumer electronics retailer Circuit City, in 2008. Most directly, electronics manufacturers held some $600 million in unpaid receivables. Indirectly, the bankruptcy created a storm of price pressure and bargain hunting as liquidators sold off discounted merchandise right in the middle of the peak Christmas buying season.

Customer response

Often, responses from customers are the most complex knock-on effects, because they may be so diverse and because so many factors are involved. Consider how buying patterns shifted when Canadians began shopping in the United States with their stronger currency in 2007–08 or the way demand declined for large sport utility vehicles and rose for compact cars and hybrids—both in response to higher fuel prices.

Applying the framework

Examining the way such risks propagate through the value chain can help management think through—imperfectly, of course—what might change fundamentally when some element in the business environment does. This analysis can have critical implications for a company's strategic decisions.

A simple analysis of direct risk, for example, suggested that one US Midwest aluminum producer would see its profits decline under new carbon regulations. Aluminum producers would be directly exposed to such regulations because the electrolysis used to extract aluminum from ore generates carbon. They're also indirectly exposed to risk from carbon because the suppliers of the electrical power needed for electrolysis generate it too. A specific aluminum producer's carbon footprint would, of course, depend on the carbon efficiency of the production process and the fuel used to generate power (hydropower, for instance, is more carbon efficient than power from coal).

Yet a different story emerges from a closer look at the supply chain, which stiffer carbon regulations would change in many different ways.

Exhibit 1: **Cascading risks**

Companies are susceptible to interconnected cascades of risk.

Exhibit 2: **Shifting advantage**

Carbon regulation would reshuffle the aluminum industry's cost curve.

Aluminum industry cost curve after factoring in cost of carbon regulation

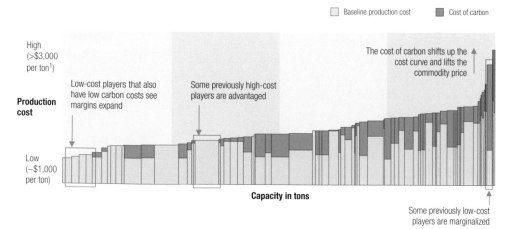

[1]Dependent on regulatory scenario.

The cost of key raw materials, such as calcined petroleum coke and caustic soda, would increase, along with logistics costs and therefore geographic premiums. The US Midwest market premium, for example, reflects the cost of delivering a ton of aluminum to the region, where demand vastly exceeds local supply. This effect favors smelters located close to the US Midwest, because they could then pocket the higher premium.

Moreover, the producer would probably benefit from added demand for aluminum—a material of choice to build lighter, more fuel-efficient cars. Since automobile manufacturing is one of the largest end markets for aluminum, carbon regulation could substantially accelerate demand, thus helping to support healthy margins and attractive new development projects. Clearly, a high carbon price would enhance aluminum's value proposition—positive news for the industry.

Finally, carbon regulations would affect not only a particular company but also its competitors, changing the economics of the business. For commodity industries like aluminum, the cash cost of marginal producers sets a floor price. In a world where carbon output has a price, the cost structure of different smelters would depend on their carbon intensity (such as the amount of carbon emitted per ton of aluminum produced) and local carbon regulations. It's possible to show how any regulatory scenario could influence the aluminum cost curve (Exhibit 2). In nearly all the plausible scenarios, the curve steepens and the floor price of aluminum therefore increases. Most industry participants, especially very carbon-efficient ones (such as those producing aluminum with hydropower), could expect a meaningful margin expansion.

For one aluminum producer that went through this mental checklist, here is the bottom line: an understanding that new carbon regulations, contrary to previous perceptions, would benefit the company thanks to its high carbon efficiency, its desirable geographic location near the US Midwest, and the potential added demand for aluminum. o

Related articles on mckinseyquarterly.com

Reducing risk in your manufacturing footprint

A supply chain CEO on the global downturn

Understanding supply chain risk: A McKinsey Global Survey

The full version of this article is available at mckinseyquarterly.com.

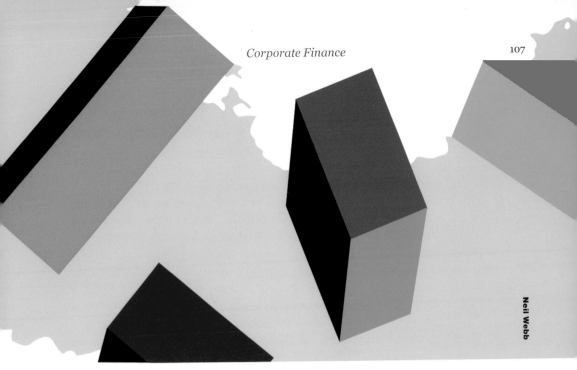

Neil Webb

Are you still the best owner of your assets?

Changes in the competitive landscape can affect an owner's distinctive advantages—and its corporate portolio. Here's how.

Richard Dobbs, Bill Huyett, and Tim Koller

The post-crisis thoughts of many executives are turning to mergers, acquisitions, and disposals. Opportunity knocks—but so does danger, and not just overpaying or selling too cheaply. The rapid pace of recovery in equity market valuations could easily make executives worry too much about being preempted by better-prepared competitors and too little about acquiring businesses where they themselves would hold a distinct advantage.

The notion that boards and management teams must understand clearly how their companies will add more value to a business than other potential owners can is a familiar one. But its importance has grown over the past year or so. Fundamental changes have swept through many industries, weakening the competitive position of deal targets and hurting the structural attractiveness of some markets. Companies also are discovering that they have lost competitive advantage in businesses they already own. These dynamics are accele-

Richard Dobbs is a director in McKinsey's Seoul office, **Bill Huyett** is a director in the Boston office, and **Tim Koller** is a principal in the New York office.

rating the rate at which a business's "better owner" changes over its life cycle.

How owners add value

Typically, a business's founders are its first best owners. As it grows, a better owner may be a venture capital firm that specializes in helping new companies thrive. Eventually, the venture capital firm may need to take the company public. As the public company grows, it might find that it can no longer compete with larger corporations because, say, it needs global distribution capabilities far beyond what it can build in a reasonable amount of time. It may thus sell itself to a larger company that's the better owner because of an existing global distribution network. As the business's market matures, the larger company may decide to sell it to a private-equity firm that could eliminate corporate overhead inconsistent with its slower growth. And once the restructuring is done, the private-equity firm can sell the division to yet another better owner: a large company that specializes in running slow-growth brands. Throughout this process, the business's better owners may add value in a number of ways.

Links to other businesses

The most straightforward way owners add value is through the links they can offer to other businesses they own, especially when such links are unique. Suppose, for instance, that a mining company has the rights to develop a coal field in a remote location far from any rail lines or other infrastructure, except for those built by another mining company, which already operates a coal mine just ten miles away. The second mining company might well be the better owner because its incremental costs to develop the mine would be lower than the first company's. It could afford to purchase the undeveloped mine at a higher price and still earn an attractive return on capital.

These unique links can occur across the value chain, from R&D and manufacturing to distribution and sales. A large pharmaceutical company with an experienced oncology sales force might, for example, be the best owner of a small pharmaceutical company with a promising new oncology drug but no sales force or commercialization capacity.

Distinctive skills

Better owners may also have distinctive and replicable functional or managerial skills. These can be found anywhere in the business system—from product development to manufacturing processes to sales and marketing—but the skill set has to be a driver of success in the industry. A company with great manufacturing skills, for example, probably wouldn't be a better owner of a consumer-packaged-goods business, because manufacturing costs aren't large enough to affect its competitive position.

In contrast, distinctive skills in developing and marketing brands often make a packaged-goods company a better owner. Take P&G, which as of 2009 had 20 brands with over $500 million in net sales and 23 with over $1 billion, all spread across a range of product categories, including laundry, beauty products, pet food, and diapers. Almost all of the billion-dollar brands rank first or second in their respective markets. What's special about P&G is that it developed these brands in different ways. Some, such as Tide and Crest, have been P&G brands for decades. Others, including Gillette and Oral-B, were acquired during the past ten years, while a number, such as Febreze and Swiffer, were developed from scratch. As a group, sales of these brands grew by 11 percent a year, on average, from 2001 through 2009.

Better governance

Owners can also add value through better governance of a business, without necessarily having a hands-on role in its day-to-day operations. Better governance refers to the way a company's owners interact with the management team to create the greatest possible long-term value; it might, for example, involve the way the owner appoints managers, structures their incentives, or challenges them on strategy. The best-performing private-equity firms excel at governance—giving them a crucial advantage over those that rely heavily on financial leverage. Indeed, prior McKinsey analysis found that in almost two-thirds of the transactions of the top-quartile funds we examined, improving the operating performance of a company relative to its peers created more value than financial leverage or good timing did.[1]

Better governance is a key reason for this outperformance. Private-equity firms govern companies very differently from the way listed companies do: for example, they typically introduce a stronger performance culture and are quick to bring in new managers when necessary. They encourage managers to abandon sacred cows and give those managers leeway to focus on improvements over a five-year horizon rather than the typical one-year time line common among listed companies. Private-equity directors also spend, on average, nearly three times as many days on their roles than directors at public companies do, and they spend most of those days on strategy and performance management rather than compliance and risk avoidance.[2]

Better insight or foresight

Companies that have insights into how a market or industry will evolve may be better owners of businesses that don't even exist yet, if

[1] Joachim Heel and Conor Kehoe, "Why some private-equity firms do better than others," mckinseyquarterly.com, February 2005. The authors analyzed 60 successful investments by 11 leading private-equity firms.
[2] Viral Acharya, Conor Kehoe, and Michael Reyner, "The voice of experience: Public versus private equity," mckinseyquarterly.com, December 2008.

they can use those insights to innovate and expand existing businesses or to develop new ones. In the 1990s, for example, Intuit noticed that many small businesses were using its Quicken software, originally designed to help individual consumers manage their personal finances. That observation led to an important insight: most accounting software was too complex for small-business owners. So Intuit designed a new product for them and within two years had claimed 80 percent of this burgeoning market.

Distinctive access to talent, capital, or relationships

This category applies primarily to companies in emerging markets, where running a business is complicated by inherently smaller pools of managerial talent, underdeveloped capital markets, and high levels of government involvement in business as customers, suppliers, and regulators. In these markets, diversified conglomerates, such as Tata and Reliance (in India) and Samsung and Hyundai (in South Korea), can be better owners because their size, stability, and relatively abundant opportunities make them more attractive employers and because they have better access to capital or distinctive relationships with governments.

Managerial implications

Executives who understand which of these distinctive advantages their company enjoys will make better-informed strategic decisions, particularly in acquiring, divesting, and negotiating the price for assets. Applying the best-owner principle can help acquirers identify targets they might normally overlook, for example. A company with, say, proven performance-improvement expertise might do better to seek out a financially weak business with great potential for betterment—rather than a business that is somehow related to its existing lines.

For divestitures, the best-owner principle allows managers to examine how the needs of the businesses they own may have evolved in different directions. It made perfect sense, for example, for diversified chemical companies to own pharmaceutical businesses 50 years ago, when their basic manufacturing and research requirements were the same. But running a profitable commodity chemical company today demands scale, operating efficiency, and the ability to manage costs and capital expenditures. By contrast, creating value in a pharmaceutical company requires a deep R&D pipeline and large local sales forces, as well as specialized expertise in areas such as the regulatory-approval process and dealing with large public and private purchasers. That is why nearly all former chemical and pharmaceutical combines have split up over the past three decades.

Understanding the best-owner principle can also help with negotiations for an acquisition, by keeping managers focused on what the target is worth specifically to their own company—as well as to other bidders. Consider the example of an Asian company bidding against a private-equity firm to purchase a European contract pharmaceutical manufacturer. The Asian company estimated the target's value to itself and also to the private-equity firm, which could add value by reducing overhead costs and attracting customers that hadn't used the target's services because it was owned by a competitor. The Asian company estimated that the contract company was worth $96 million to the private-equity firm.

Related articles on mckinseyquarterly.com

When to break up a conglomerate: An interview with Tyco International's CFO

Creating value: The debate over public vs. private ownership

The Asian company could make the same overhead cost reductions and add similar customers—but on top of this, it could move some of the manufacturing to its lower-cost plants. As a result, the target's value to the Asian company was $120 million, so it was the best owner and could pay a higher price than the private-equity firm would, while still capturing significant value. As a side note, the value of the target to its European parent was only $80 million.

Knowing the relative values, the Asian company could afford to bid, say, $100 million, pushing out the private-equity firm and gaining $20 million in potential value creation. By announcing plans to enter the business even without making the acquisition, the Asian company could further increase its share of the value to be captured. If the seller and the private-equity firm were convinced, they would have to reduce their estimates of the target's value, and the Asian company could reduce its bid, capturing more value still.

The payoff for the Asian company that applied these principles was avoiding the trap of conducting negotiations right up to its own breakeven point. Instead of asking how much the company could pay, its executives were able to identify the least they needed to pay to win the deal and create the most value. o

The authors would like to thank Chris Bradley for his contributions to this article and John Stuckey, who led McKinsey's earlier thinking on best ownership.

We welcome your comments on this article. Please send them to quarterly_comments@mckinsey.com.

This article is excerpted and adapted from the authors' forthcoming book, *Value: The Four Cornerstones of Corporate Finance* (Boston: John Wiley and Sons, 2010).

The full version of this article is available at mckinseyquarterly.com.

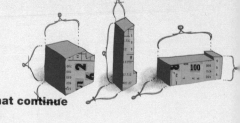

Enduring Ideas

Classic McKinsey frameworks that continue to inform management thinking

Valuation and value creation

Growth and return on invested capital (ROIC) generate value

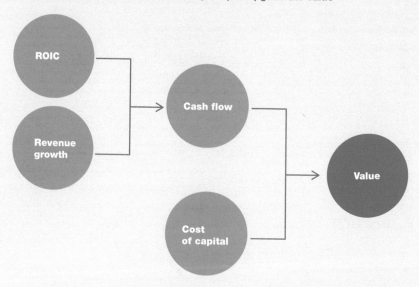

Companies thrive when they create real economic value for their shareholders. Although the fundamental approach to measuring its creation has held steady for decades, McKinsey brought the 'numbers' together with the strategic context of companies, creating a tight link between their value and their competitive position and strategy. In *Valuation: Measuring and Managing the Value of Companies* (first edition, 1990), authors Tom Copeland, Tim Koller, and Jack Murrin called upon businesses to quantify the value their strategic decisions create, so that they can identify the best options.

Many executives make the mistake of focusing solely on earnings as the measure of value creation. Yet the evidence shows that the ability to generate long-term cash flows is what actually drives it. Furthermore, as the accompanying framework illustrates, cash flows are derived from both returns on invested capital (ROIC) and revenue growth. What's more, those cash flows—adjusted for the cost of capital, to reflect the time value of money and the risk of future flows—constitute a company's value.

This principle continues to guide managers who aim to create long-term value for their companies. By observing the interactions between returns on capital and growth, corporate leaders can examine the impact of changes in either category on the value of their companies. In general, those with high returns on capital generate more value from growth. Those with low returns generate more value by increasing them than by continuing to grow. **o**